TOWARDS A THEOLOGY FOR INTER-FAITH DIALOGUE

Inter-Anglican Publishing Network

Australia

Anglican Information Office
St Andrew's House
Sydney Square
Sydney 2000

Canada

Anglican Book Centre
600 Jarvis Street
Toronto, Ontario M4Y 2J6

Ghana

Anglican Press Ltd
PO Box 8
Accra

Kenya

Uzima Press Ltd
PO Box 48127
Nairobi

New Zealand

Genesis
29 Westminster Street
PO Box 22-537
Christchurch

Nigeria

CSS Press
50 Broad Street
PO Box 174
Lagos

Southern and Central Africa

Collins Liturgical Publications
Distributed in Southern
Africa by
Lux Verbi, PO Box 1822
Cape Town 8000

Tanzania

Central Tanganyika Press
PO Box 15
Dodoma

Uganda

Centenary Publishing House
PO Box 2776
Kampala

United Kingdom

Church House Publishing
Church House
Great Smith Street
London SW1P 3NZ

United States of America

Forward Movement Publications
412 Sycamore Street
Cincinnati, Ohio 45202

TOWARDS A THEOLOGY FOR INTER-FAITH DIALOGUE

PUBLISHED FOR THE
ANGLICAN CONSULTATIVE COUNCIL

First published 1984 for the Board for Mission and Unity of the General Synod of the Church of England by CIO Publishing.

Second edition, with additional material and revised bibliography, published for the Anglican Consultative Council, 14 Great Peter Street, London SW1P 3NQ.

This edition by
Church House Publishing
Church House, Great Smith Street
London SW1P 3NZ

ISBN 0 7151 5525 3

Printed by Orphans Press Ltd., Hereford Road, Leominster, Herefordshire.

CONTENTS

FREEDOM OF THE SPIRIT

O Holy Spirit, whose presence is liberty:
Grant me that freedom of the Spirit,
which will not fear to tread in unknown ways
nor be held back
by fear of others or misgivings of ourselves.
Ever beckon us forward
to the place of thy will
which is also the place of thy power,
O ever-leading, ever-loving Lord.

George Appleton
One Man's Prayers
SPCK second ed. 1977 p.19.

FOREWORD

As the title indicates, the report *Towards a Theology for Inter-Faith Dialogue* was written as an exploration into a new and sensitive area for Christians in England. The group who prepared this report were conscious that this was the beginning of a journey and that any theology which was written had to be provisional. The subsequent debate in the General Synod of the Church of England in July 1984 fully justified their hope.

Since that time there have been responses received from numerous individuals and groups of people. The essay which comes from Pakistan and from a very different cultural milieu was written by the Rt Revd Michael J. Nazir-Ali, until recently Bishop of Raiwind, and has been added to this reprint. Christopher Wright contributed a critical essay to the magazine *Anvil,* Vol. 1 No. 3 (1984), which ran parallel to Christopher Sugden's *Christ's Exclusive Claims and Inter-Faith Dialogue* in the Grove Booklet No. 22 (1985).

Further afield, the report has been noted by both the World Council of Churches and the Vatican. We are grateful that what was seen as the first mile in a journey of exploration has been taken up by so many. It is now offered to all the dioceses of the Anglican Communion for study and reflection in preparation for the Lambeth Conference 1988. Following such study we look forward to the bishops taking us on the next stage of the journey.

There lies before us a vision of the unity of humankind under God: a vision which both St Paul and St John hint at in the New Testament, a unity which is rich and diverse, and has so much to do with the issue of peace and justice for the world in which we live. May God grant us that spirit of discernment that we may do his will.

BARRY BRISTOL
The Rt Revd Barry Rogerson
Chairman, Inter-Faith Consultative Group
Board for Mission and Unity, Church of England

SAMUEL VAN CULIN
Secretary General
The Anglican Consultative Council
and Secretary to the Lambeth Conference

PREFACE TO FIRST EDITION

This report is the work of the Inter-Faith Consultative Group of the Board for Mission and Unity:

The Bishop of Wolverhampton (Chairman)

The Rev. Bernard Chamberlain CR	Mr. Alan Brown (Board of Education)
Mrs Valerie Fisher	
The Rev. Christopher Lamb	The Rev. Kenneth Cracknell (BCC)
Miss Marie Lewis	The Rev. William Jacob (ACCM)
The Rev. Alan Race	The Rev. Kenneth Leech (BSR)
	The Rev. Canon Eric Reid (Hospital Chaplaincies)

Mrs Mary Tanner (BMU) (Secretary)

The Report was initiated by Bishop David Brown, whose knowledge and experience in the sphere of inter-faith relations was outstanding, and both the Group and the Board wish to acknowledge his contribution to it. As well as being Chairman of the Board for Mission and Unity, Bishop David was Chairman of the BCC Committee on Relations with People of Other Faiths which, with its Secretary, the Rev. Kenneth Cracknell, produced *Guidelines for Dialogue in Britain*. This paper on the theological issues involved in dialogue is submitted in response to a request of the General Synod.

The Board is grateful to the Group, and in particular to its Chairman, the Rt Rev. Barry Rogerson and to its Secretary, Mary Tanner, for the careful work they have done and for the challenge they have presented. The exploration is new and the area is a sensitive one. Not all the members of the Board are able to agree with all that has been written. Nevertheless the Board recognises the Report as an important contribution to an ongoing debate in which the whole Church in this country needs to engage.

The Board commends this Report for study, reflection and debate.

DAPHNE WALES
Chairman of the Board for Mission and Unity

INTRODUCTION

1.   In November 1981 the General Synod considered the British Council of Churches' *Guidelines for Dialogue*.[1] It commended to the dioceses as 'a guide for action' the four principles set out there as a basis on which people of different religions can live and work harmoniously together in one community.[2] At the same time the General Synod asked the Board for Mission and Unity to prepare a report on 'the theological aspects of dialogue'. In the time between the Synod's request and the appearance of this paper it has become more evident that the Church is being asked to direct thinking and to take a prophetic lead in the area of inter-faith relations. Christians are genuinely perplexed by the unfamiliar and disturbing questions raised in their everyday relations with those of other faiths. The discussion of specific questions in the General Synod, particularly the debate on the sale of church properties to those of other faiths, has confirmed the need to stimulate widespread reflection on the underlying theological issues.[3] Furthermore, the work of the Board of Education on guidelines in education in a multi-cultural context, the publication of a booklet by the Church of England Hospital Chaplaincies Council on the ministry of hospital chaplains in a multi-faith society and the appearance of the British Council of Churches' booklet *Can We Pray Together?* underline the need for theological reflection.[4]

2.   Theological reflection ought not to be undertaken in the abstract. It must engage with the experience of those whose lives are daily caught up in inter-faith situations. The insights of Scripture and Tradition have to be related to experience, so that experience may speak to Scripture and Tradition. At the same time it is to be expected that Scripture and Tradition will sometimes confirm and sometimes judge what is perceived in experience. Exploration of the theological aspects of dialogue must not be left only to those who live in multi-faith situations nor to the theologians. The reflection is the responsibility of the whole Christian community open to the guidance of the Spirit.

3.   Nor should the Church of England undertake this alone, but, on the Lund Principle, must work together with other ecumenical partners. Indeed the Board for Mission and Unity has always insisted on working closely with the BCC's Committee for Relations with People of Other Faiths. This Committee provides an important forum for the British Churches to explore and act together. Again we welcome and have used in the preparation of this paper reports from the World Council of Churches, including the reflections of the Vancouver Assembly, as well as the recent work of the Vatican Secretariat for non-Christians.[5]

4.   In what follows we take account of the changed context in which British Christians find themselves and attempt to describe the range of views held by Christians on the activity of God in the world as that affects the understanding of other faiths. There follows a consideration of biblical and theological pointers which we believe should direct us in understanding our appropriate relationship to those of other faiths. Finally we turn to elucidate what seems to us to be implied in what is currently termed 'dialogue'. In particular we explore the four guidelines already accepted by the General Synod. In such a new area our thinking is tentative and exploratory. We hope that others will join us in reflecting upon what has been called elsewhere 'a wider ecumenism'.

A CHANGED CONTEXT

5.   The Gospel was rooted in Judaism and the Old Testament, but the apostles proclaimed it in the Hellenistic world of the Roman Empire, and the Fathers developed their theology in the context of Greek and Roman cults and philosophies. From the seventh century onwards, Christians and Muslims have been in contact with each other throughout the Near East, Western Asia and Spain, and in Europe Jews have for centuries lived alongside Christians. Christianity was early in touch with Hinduism in India, and from the seventh to the fourteenth century AD, through the Nestorian churches, with Buddhism and Chinese traditions in Central Asia and China. The Western Church developed an aggressive crusading ethos, the effects of which are hard to be free from even today. During the last four centuries of missionary endeavour, contacts with these other religions of Asia have greatly increased, while in Africa, America (both North and South) and the Pacific, the Gospel has been preached against the background of traditional religions.

6.   Contacts between Christianity and other major world religions have, therefore, been both long and varied, even though the number of people involved were few. Until recently the tendency was for religious groups to keep very much to themselves. Most people lived their whole lives within their own communities with very little contact with those who differed from them. However, in recent years the situation has changed.

7.   There are many forces and influences that have made a new relationship possible. Some of these have happened on the global level, and Britain, perhaps, more than any other country, has been affected by the international changes that have taken place since the end of the second world war. In 1945 London was still the metropolis of a vast empire, and counted as subjects of His Majesty were nearly all the Hindus in the world, all the Sikhs, a vast proportion of the Muslims, and enormous numbers of Buddhists. In 1945 our great missionary societies were still at work in China, in Burma and in many other lands now closed to us. No visas or residence permits were required for India or Nigeria. Bangladesh, Ghana and Zimbabwe and a score of other lands had not been conceived. The connection between Christian mission and the colonial Government was still intact, despite ominous cracks beginning to appear, for India was already on the way to independence in 1947.

8.   At home civil virtues and ethical idealism were linked with Christianity, and the 1944 Education Act had just come into force. Spencer Leeson, later to be Bishop of Peterborough, wrote at the time: 'Parliament has declared the will of the nation that it shall be a Christian nation; and the State-aided schools are to do their part by teaching the

nation's children to worship and to understand'. The collective daily act of worship in every state maintained school and religious instruction remain the two activities required by law in our school system to this present time, but nowhere in the framing of the Act does it say that it shall be Christian worship or Christian religious teaching. This vision of one nation under God continues to sustain many people today. And yet the situation is very different. Both the religious map of the world and the demographic patterns of the people of these islands have changed beyond all imagination.

9.   Within living memory every religion tended to be restricted to specific parts of the world. If one wished to see Buddhism at first-hand it was necessary to travel to Ceylon or Japan. Now the Chiswick Vihara has some twenty thousand people on its mailing list, and saffron-robed monks walk the Sussex lanes or the streets of Wolverhampton. A Japanese peace pagoda rises on a lakeside in Milton Keynes and another is to tower above the western suburbs of London. Muslims lived, then, in Arabia over-spilling into North Africa, and eastwards into Persia and India. (Even then our ideas were restricted, few of us realizing that Indonesia was to become the largest Muslim nation.) Now among Nash's terraces surrounding Regent's Park the great dome of a splendid mosque symbolizes the presence of nearly a million Muslims in the United Kingdom - most of whom are not exotic visitors from oil rich states but fellow-citizens with us. They make vital contributions to Britain's economic well-being and social life. So even Church Schools in some Northern and Midland cities now may be almost entirely composed of Muslim pupils. Hindus were properly the citizens of the Indian Empire (indeed, their name signifies not so much their religious beliefs as the land to which they belonged). Now Leicester has the largest Hindu community, after Durban, outside India; and Birmingham and Wolverhampton, Manchester and Leeds, Coventry and Bristol, as well as dozens of much smaller towns, have flourishing temples and celebrate Hindu festivals like *diwali*. Sikhs, too, have left their ancestral homes in north-west India, or have been expelled by various regimes from their adopted countries in East Africa. Some two hundred thousand of these 'disciples' (for this is what the word 'Sikh' means) are now settled in Britain: the Woolwich *gurdwara* (just one example) counts its adherents as fifteen thousand. Nor should we forget the Chinese 'diaspora' scattered the length and breadth of these islands. New research is discovering how much of the old religions of China is still being practised among them. There are, too, smaller communities of Jains, of Zoroastrians, and of Baha'is, many of these last refugees from the appalling persecutions taking place in modern Iran. But even this is not all of the story. For in another sense Britain has been a multi-religious society, at least since we ceased trying to expel the

Jews from these islands. The Board of Deputies estimates that there are 385,000 Jews living in the UK, and their positive contribution to all aspects of British life is unquestionable.[6]

10. So the religious map is altered, in the world and in our own country. We need only note here that our British experience is paralleled in every Western European country; nearly six million Muslims live in Common Market countries. It is matched too in Canada and in South Africa, both Toronto and Durban claim to be the most multi-religious cities in the world, and of course in the USA.

11. In Britain, as in many other countries, Christians, Muslims, Hindus and people of other faiths work together in the same shops, offices and factories, study together in the same schools and colleges, travel on the same buses and trains, work together in the same hospitals and public services, pay the same taxes and are represented by the same Members of Parliament. Many people find this religious and cultural mixture a novel and bewildering experience. Not only Christians, but people of other faiths as well, find it strange to work as colleagues or be neighbours with people who hold different beliefs and observe different customs, who keep different religious festivals and holidays, and who profess allegiance to different religious teachers. Sometimes Christians admire the devotion and loyalty to their faith of those of other religions. They are challenged by the deep springs of faith, wisdom and spirituality, the willingness to accept the demanding rules and discipline of their faith and the close fellowship and commitment to the family, often the extended family, that characterises the lives of others. In all this they challenge Christians to rethink their own beliefs and practices. More often, however, differences and strangeness divides and alienates the different religious communities. Genuine fear of that which is strange develops, sometimes leading to extreme behaviour as one community seeks to exclude and hurt that which it does not understand and which it can only perceive in terms of a threat. Rivalries and jealousies between groups lead to violence which destroys any possibility of living with creative diversity.

12. The situation in which relationships between those of different religious persuasions have to be worked out is delicate and complicated. The fact that those of other cultures and religions are British citizens, with the same rights, privileges and duties, is an important change in the context. It is no longer with someone out there, at a distance, that we engage in conversation, but with those with whom we share in a way quite other than any previous generation. Nevertheless, we ought not to minimize the fact that numerically those of other faiths are few compared with the number of practising Christians in Britain. The relative size of communities has a profound effect on our self-understanding, and

conditions the way we relate to others. Adherents of different faiths seldom meet as equals, and isolation and cultural dominance are hard to overcome.

13.   However, Christians share with those of other faiths an awareness of, and a search for, 'the Other', 'the ground of all being', though they use very different language, symbols and imagery to express it. This is a powerful witness to draw those of different faiths nearer to each other. Together they can challenge contemporary life-styles in the West, largely secularist in attitude, with its emphasis upon material goods and values.

14.   This movement of peoples, these alterations in the religious map, have taken place with astonishing rapidity, within the lifetime of most worshipping members of the Church of England. The contemporary experience of Christianity as one religion among others presents a new challenge for the Church. Christians are now required to express their specific witness afresh in the light of the new knowledge which increased contact with other religious traditions brings. It is a challenge which must be accepted by the Church if Christian witness is to be dynamic, able to engage fruitfully within a changed context. In these circumstances, Christian theologians are turning away from a tendency to dismiss other religions and are searching for appropriate ways of responding to their persistent presence. But if that relationship is to mean more than merely peaceful co-existence or being nice to one another it has to be based upon a theological understanding of the activity of God in the world. At this point in the history of the Church we detect a variety of theories about how other religions accord with the Christian understanding of God. These various views each determine significantly different modes of relating to those of other faiths. It is such views which we detect under-lying the conflicting speeches and voting patterns that have marked the work of the General Synod in recent years.

15.   We recognise that there are positions at either end of a broad spectrum of views that would not allow for any dialogue with those of other faiths: on the one hand the extreme exclusivist view which claims there is nothing to be learnt in dialogue with others and, on the other, the extreme relativist view which sees no need for mission and evangelism. We make no attempt in what follows to engage with such positions. But within these two extremes the range of opinion embraces those positions which may be categorised as exclusivism, inclusivism and pluralism. These do not represent rigidly tight categories. Each carries within itself different emphases. Few of us think only within one category but move between them. Nevertheless it is useful to describe these positions in order to understand the differing positions which issue in different behaviour and attitude to those of other faiths.

(i)   Exclusivism

16.   At one end of the spectrum the Christian exclusivist theory counts all religions other than Christianity as the product of blindness or even sinful unbelief. At the very extreme this is expressed by saying that they are the work of Satan. At best, other religions represent the fruit of God's activity in nature and conscience, which is distorted by sin or human

pride. Consequently, they are either wholly in error, or simply inadequate for salvation, and reflect nothing of the real saving grace of God. On this understanding the doctrine of the Incarnation of Christ places Christianity in opposition to, or discontinuous with the other religions. Christ alone is the Saviour who has revealed perfectly the heart and mind of the Father, and the true way of discipleship. Those who do not acknowledge this word of truth therefore stand under judgement. Moreover this judgement applies equally to the Church, when it is seen to be acting without reliance on God's grace given in the Incarnation. For Exclusivism, then, the absolute supremacy of Christ is a given part of the data of Christian identity.

17.   On this view any relation with those of other faiths is primarily for the purpose of witnessing to the revelation of God in Jesus Christ with little expectation, if any, of gain or enlightenment in return. The intention is that the other partner will be converted to the Christian way. If it is allowed that there are insights which do not contradict or compromise the Christian understanding of God they are only acceptable when purified in the light of faith in Christ.

(ii)   Inclusivism

18.   As a result of the realisation that a great spiritual depth is found in many of the religious traditions of the world and that they show all the signs of persisting in the future, many theologians are turning to a more positive account of the place of other religions within a Christian understanding of the activity of God. While holding firmly to the belief that God was supremely manifest in Jesus, inclusivist theories also affirm the universal presence of God's Spirit through the whole of creation. God's saving power and presence is defined in the life, death and resurrection of Jesus, but it is not confined to him. Through his Logos or his Spirit, God is operative beyond Christian culture, bringing salvation to other peoples and cultures who may not even know the name of Jesus. This is not to say that Christianity is on an equal footing with other religions. The supremacy of the Christian way is retained in one of two ways. First, Christ is held to be the indisputable author of salvation because this is a given part of Christian identity (this givenness of the person of Christ is similar to that in Exclusivism). The relationship between Christianity and the other religions is then analogous to the traditional Christian judgement on its own Jewish heritage. As Judaism became interpreted as a preparation for the greater light of the Gospel, so the other religions are seen as forerunners of the Gospel. Some inclusivists would wish to underline more strongly than others the special place of Judaism among the forerunners of the Gospel as witnessing to a special divine disclosure and redemptive activity. The revelation of God in Christ is the concrete,

historical form of what remains hidden in the depths of other religions. A second way of asserting Christian supremacy is by speaking of the normativeness of Jesus and the Christian way when this is compared with other ways. Jesus is supremely the standard or correct measure by which other religious experience must be judged. This assertion of Christian supremacy is arrived at after an historical comparison of the truths and fruits of the religious experience of the major world faiths.

19.   Inclusivist theory stresses how Christianity does in fact complete other forms of religion. As the New Testament writers searched the Jewish Scriptures (what we have come to call the Old Testament), for signs of Christ before his incarnation in the person of Jesus, so the same can be done in relation to other religions. They too have their teachers, prophets, holy people and scriptures. Moreover the spiritual truths found there are more readily and thankfully embraced on this inclusivist account than with the exclusivist outlook.

(iii)   Pluralism[7]

20.   The shift from an exclusive to an inclusive view of the place of other religions within a Christian understanding of the universal love of God is now common among many theologians. However there are a growing number who favour a further move in the direction of what can be termed Pluralism. Proponents of this theory argue that the different religions present different images of God which represent different experiences of the divine life spread abroad in history and culture. This is not to say that all religions are ultimately the same, or equally true. Such a conclusion lies at the other end of the range of opinion in the theology of religions. This theory, understood more positively, simply states that the differences between religions arise from the different human interpretations of the revelation of the one God according to cultural limitations. It acknowledges the historical observation that religions have flourished in relative independence in the past. Also it claims to take more seriously the incompleteness of any one revelation (the symbol for this in Christianity is the Second Coming). Some Christians can assent to this theory because they believe that the full, true and reliable revelation of God in Christ may not necessarily entail a belief in his ultimate supremacy. Christianity is absolute in so far as it calls for a full commitment to the way of Jesus, a commitment which has universal relevance, but does not claim to exhaust the mystery of divine truth. Thus Pluralism leaves open the question whether any one religion can claim the supremacy of religious truth prior to the dialogue between religions proper.

21.   Those who hold the pluralist view will be concerned with the way other religions might be brought into some kind of larger ecumenical

relationship where the truths of each are seen as complementary to each other. Christianity's witness to Jesus as normative for all people is retained by some pluralists but it does not foreclose the possibility that there might be other norms which contribute to a larger picture of the work of God in the world.

22.   With such a range of opinion lying behind inter-faith matters it is no wonder that there is much uncertainty and difference of opinion about correct action in any specific circumstance affecting relations between Christians and those of other faiths. The situation is further complicated when we recognise that all of these three positions embody subtle differences within themselves so that the overall range of the Christian response to the other religions is more complex even than the picture painted here. Another complicating factor is that none of our individual emphases can account for, or be fitted easily into, broadly defined positions. Many of us tend to move from one emphasis to another within ourselves. So we must acknowledge at this juncture in the Church's history that there is no agreed consensus about how to proceed in relation to other religions. There is, however, some common ground shared by advocates of all three positions though hardly between the hardliners of the exclusivist and pluralist positions. Many would agree that relations with other faiths include witnessing to the Christian centrality of the work and person of Jesus, being prepared to let go of much of the cultural packaging of the Gospel as we strive to express the Christian revelation in other cultural forms, and a willingness to learn to some degree from other witnesses and religious traditions. But what is at issue is truth: what has to be retained at all costs and what can be surrendered for the sake of better, richer things and deeper understandings? This is what we are being forced to consider in the light of our new experience and knowledge of other religions. The point at which there is greatest dis-agreement is whether the essential Christian identity automatically entails the supremacy of Christian belief and life over all other systems of belief and action. Only when we begin to understand where as a Christian community and where as individual members of that community we stand on such questions shall we begin to live confidently, without fear, in the new situation of a multi-faith society.

23.   And so we turn to the biblical witness for guidance and to the insights of the Christian tradition to discover there pointers which help to determine what content we may give to the relatively new concept of 'dialogue' and to the four guidelines for dialogue already endorsed by the General Synod.

24.   In seeking to understand the appropriate relationship of Christians to those of other faiths we have been driven back to ask what guidance we can take from Scripture. While believing firmly in Scripture as the primary source of authority for the Christian community we cannot accept that an answer to this, or any other contemporary puzzle, is to be discovered in any single quotation or any one strand of biblical thought. We refuse to wrest any biblical quotation from its context and use it as a sole basis for determining our attitude towards those of other faiths. Any biblical quotation has to be understood against its own immediate context, and also against the burden of the entire biblical message. Furthermore, the Scriptures have been given to the community of the Church and their interpretation belongs within the whole community. Neither professional theologians, indispensable as their work of interpretation is, nor ordained ministers, with their special role as guardians of the Tradition, are the sole arbiters in interpreting the Bible. Only when the broadest community, lay and ordained, professional and non-professional, women and men, bring their lived experience and insight into the interpretative or hermeneutical process can the authoritative word be most nearly perceived. Only then can the gulf be bridged between what the Scriptures said and what they say now to the present-day community of faith. The authority of Scripture stands in relation to the community. Led by the Spirit, with the special guidance of theologians and ordained ministers, the community will discover new and authoritative insights in the old stories and words. Once we have rejected the authority of any single text, whether from Old Testament or New Testament, to guide us in developing a theology of inter-faith dialogue, we are left to discover how the Bible as a whole can act as the primary authoritative source. What guidance can we take in seeking to answer the puzzles emerging in new and challenging ways in our generation in relations between Christians and those of other faiths? Here, as in other areas, the Bible provides no blueprint or model and yet we believe it provides a compass which can direct us. Both the process of the formation of the biblical witness as well as the individual theological insights about the nature of God and God's relation to his creation suggest certain implications for our relationship with those of other faiths.[8]

25.   Behind the complex witness of the Old and New Testaments, modern scholarship points to a pattern of revelation which is important for inter-faith dialogue. The Old Testament is made up of a diversity of literature covering almost 2,000 years in which many theologians, historians, wisdom writers, psalmists, prophets, testify to a belief in God. We see them wrestling consciously, or unconsciously, with the traditions which they had inherited about God and his relation with his covenant people. They do this in the light of their own experience of their contemporary religious, historical and political conditions in the midst of foreign cultures and alien religious traditions. In such a process they did not simply reiterate their traditions but were responsible for recreating the tradition with new and significant insights. So the tradition, their vision of the nature and being of God and humanity, was never static but alive and growing, and ever tested by the community of Israel that received it. In the first five books of the Old Testament we glimpse the way a number of Israelites, over the course of several centuries, interpreted their foundation events, the patriarchal and Exodus events, the unique tradition that belonged to their nation, in an attempt to make that past speak to the present. The book of Deuteronomy is the clearest example of this. Similarly, reflection on the past tradition and its relevance for the present, is continued in the declarations of the prophets as they seek to understand the implications of election and covenant in their contemporary situation, in the Psalmists as they celebrate Israel's calling, and by the wisdom writers who concentrate on the way of response. Throughout is the overwhelming conviction that whatever such preachers and writers were doing in handling their tradition and reforming it, was forced on them, often against their will, by the Spirit of God.[9]

26.   In the same way we see the writers of the New Testament, over a much shorter period, wrestling with the traditions which they in their turn had received: the complex traditions of the Old Testament and Judaism. What marks the New Testament off from the Old is that those inherited traditions are measured against what the evangelists and letter writers perceived about Jesus of Nazareth, the one they recognised as the decisive and unique intervention of God in history, to which the Old Testament had looked forward. We can see the New Testament writers, like those of the Old, interpreting their inheritance again in light of their experience. One of the most remarkable facts that emerges is the degree of freedom which each writer exercised in handling what was inherited. It is the very freedom with which they used their material that gave rise to the creative diversity of biblical witness.

27.   This process of revelation in both Testaments witnesses to a dialogue between the inherited and the contemporary experience of the individual and the community. A part of that contemporary experience which is brought to bear on the tradition is the experience of other cultures and other religions. This is most clearly seen in the long period of Old Testament history in the effects of Egyptian, Canaanite, Assyrian, Babylonian, Persian and Greek cultures and religions on Israel's understanding of the nature and being of God.

28.   One of the most obvious examples of this is the effect that the views of sacral kingship of surrounding nations had upon Israel's understanding and expression of monarchy, contributing so much in the process to the messianic concept as it emerged later in Israel's history.[10] Another moving example of the effects of openness to other traditions is seen remarkably at the very point when the prophet Hosea is decrying most strongly the Baalim of Canaan.[11] In his polemic against the fertility cults, he takes over the language and the imagery he is attacking and re-applies it in the most daring and startling of ways to Yahweh and his bride, Israel. Again in its initial development the teaching of wisdom in Israel owed much to the wisdom schools of other contemporary peoples. Indeed, the editor of Kings does not hesitate to compare the wisdom of Solomon with that of other peoples.[12] And the personification of wisdom, pre-existent beside God at creation, agent in creation, though never independent of Yahweh owed much to what was drawn from foreign sources.[13] This was to become important in understanding both the doctrine of creation and of the Trinity.

29.   Similarly this pattern of relationship between Israel and other cultures and other religions which becomes more evident when the Old Testament is set against its contemporary background is no less discernible in the New Testament. The prologue to John's Gospel, the Epistle to the Hebrews and many of the letters of Paul show the effects of Greek and Roman culture and thought patterns in the interpretative process of the life, death and resurrection of Jesus.[14] Paul's speech to the Court of Areopagus at Athens in Acts 17 provides a clear example of the way in which the apostles shared the news of Christ with educated people of the Hellenistic and Roman cities. It contains allusions to Stoic and Epicurean philosophy and quotes with approval a well-known poem. The inference is that Paul and his colleagues were eager to use their knowledge of current philosophies and to find whatever common ground they could with their audiences in order to share the Gospel message.

30.   The history of the Old Israel, as well as the New, points to a pattern of engagement with other cultures and other religions: an engagement never without opposition, conflict and threat, as the prophets clearly show.

Nevertheless the insights and perspectives of other cultures and religions, when brought into proximity with the tradition of Israel, often led to new and creative insights into the nature of God, of his relationship to Israel and through Israel to the world. It is when Israel is most open to others that she is most creative. On the contrary in the post-exilic period the policy of exclusiveness and isolation, admittedly adopted to protect and safeguard, turned out to have an impoverishing effect.

31.   Our contemporary situation in Britain in relation to those of other faiths is significantly different from any previous age. And yet there is surely much to be discovered in studying the process of the formation of biblical witness to suggest that openness to others, not isolation, is the way to new insights into the nature and being of God and of God's desire for, and demands upon, his creation. But more than this, the Bible also provides essential pointers in the unfolding witness to the Triune God, Creator, Redeemer and Sustainer, and in its testimony to the inner life of God, the Trinity, which can guide us in inter-faith relations.

(i)   The Creating God

32.   The Bible begins with an impressive statement of faith in God, the Creator of heaven and earth. This is never denied in all that follows. The least that can be said is that the relation of created to Creator is shared by all peoples. Throughout the Bible the relationship of Creator to those he creates claims the attention of biblical writers. The Isaianic disciple of the exile is convinced without doubt that Yahweh is the only God and seeks to show that this creator God is the one who desires that his righteousness and salvation should be taken to the furthest isles, to the ends of the earth. He sees the nations coming to worship God on Mount Zion: all creatures subject to their Creator. But between the creation, at the beginning of time, and the consummation of all things is the age of sin and death, the consequence of human free will. Separation from God, darkness and sin, are as much a part of the reality of life as beauty and joy. This dark side of life is part of the context in which all relationships have to be lived out and redeemed. We all share in the fallenness of humanity. No earthly relationship, however loving, is without cost or pain. This is part of the dynamic of history: it is there throughout the Old Testament: it is there focused and entered into most deeply on the Cross. And, although the outcome is assured by the Cross and Resurrection, conflict and alienation continue as integral to the human condition.

(ii)   The Covenanting God

33.   The story of the Old Testament and the New Testament is of the Creator God who desires to be in relationship with his creatures. This relationship is expressed in the biblical concept of covenant. Although most of the Old Testament is concerned with the covenant between God and Israel it is not, as is often believed, this exclusive covenant which is either prior or primary. The context of the whole Bible is given in Genesis 1. God is the Creator of all things and gives humanity a charge to take dominion. The sign of this Adamic covenant is the sabbath. Similarly the covenant with Noah embraces all humanity and indeed all creation. The covenant with Abraham is in order that all peoples shall be blessed. It is only within the universal framework of relationship that the biblical writers set the particular covenant with Israel. To understand the covenants with Adam, Noah and Abraham as primary rather than the Mosaic covenant, leads to a dramatically different reading of the Old Testament and points the direction of salvation history in a different way. It leads to the recognition that all humanity is the people of God and that the God of the Jewish and Christian revelation is the God of all peoples. This is further hinted at within the Old Testament. 'Have not I brought the

Philistines from Caphtor and the Syrians from Kir?' (Amos 9.7). Moreover the Assyrians and Egyptians are not related to God indirectly through Israel, but directly (Isaiah 19.25). However the particular historical developments of the post-exilic period led Israel to a more exclusive view of things. The Mosaic covenant was interpreted in terms of the separation of the Holy People for God with little emphasis on Israel's vocation to the world. This was dramatically overturned in the New Testament. By the life, death and resurrection of Jesus all, Jew and Gentile, slave and free, women and men are brought potentially within the relationship of the new covenant. Chapter 2 of Ephesians explains this most clearly. The Gentiles, 'strangers to the covenants of promise' and 'far off' have been brought near in the blood of Christ. The Church is the new Israel, its membership open to all. Here is the reversal of the post-exilic process of exclusivism to that potentially inclusive relation inherent in creation. The goal of all history and of all peoples is set in the direction of a 'mended creation' and a restored relation between the Creator and all that he creates.

(iii) The Electing God

34. In the Bible the notion of covenant is closely bound up with the idea of election. God calls Israel in her weakness in Egypt into a peculiar relationship with himself: 'I will be your God and you shall be my people'. Israel is called to be a 'kingdom of priests', 'a holy people'. The prophets of the Old Testament are clear that this has nothing to do with merit but depends entirely upon the gracious calling and the continuing forgiving acts of God. They saw most clearly that election and the particularity of the Mosaic covenant relationship was for a purpose and not an end in itself. Israel was called 'to know' God and to hold that knowledge in trust for the rest of the world. One of the most profound illustrations of this comes in the first of the so-called 'servant poems', reflections of the Isaianic prophet of the exile. The servant, Israel, is called by God for mission, to bring judgement and justice to the furthest coasts, all the inhabited world. The servant is not powerful in worldly terms, not oppressive or coercive: vulnerable and wounded he carries out his task. His mission is carried out by seeking in others that which is of worth and true. He is to draw that out and not extinguish it however dimly it burns: 'the bruised reed he shall not break, the smouldering flax he shall not quench' (Isaiah 42.3).

35. By the time of the New Testament this prophetic conception of election was obscured. Many, but not all, rabbis instead of teaching that Israel's vocation was to the service of the nations reversed this. They claimed that the world was created for the sake of Israel and there was no question of the salvation of the Gentiles.

'O Lord ... for our sakes thou madest the world. As for the other nations, which also came of Adam, thou hast said that they are nothing, and are like unto spittle ... And now, O Lord, behold, these nations, which are reputed as nothing, be lords over us and devour us. If the world be made for our sakes, why do we not possess for an inheritance our world? How long shall this endure?'

(II (4) Esdras 6.55-59)

Many Jews of the New Testament period believed that their election and their covenant with God implied that only they were the centre and object of God's activity in creation and redemption and that they had no responsibility for the Gentiles. Such exclusivist beliefs were powerful and hard to overturn. They have continued to echo within the Christian tradition.

36.   But the New Testament attacks this distorted view and returns to the principles of election in the earlier tradition. God rejects the elect and calls a new people out of all nations. The Gentiles are included in God's saving purpose. This is 'the purpose of God according to election' (Romans 9.11). Election is the work of divine grace, which works in history to accomplish God's ultimate purpose. There is little or no emphasis on the election of the individual. Emphasis is upon the social aspect of election. Election refers to God's purposes in this world. It is true that the elected ones, if they do not fall away, will indeed be saved in the world to come, but that is not the primary meaning of election. Nothing is implied about the rejection of any individuals. The New Testament never teaches that any human beings have been created for reprobation, or that they are now irredeemably predestined to damnation. Indeed, it was precisely against such a view - the rabbinic notion of the rejection of the 'other nations' - that the Christian movement was a protest. In the Old Testament election is a matter of service and not of privilege.

37.   Thus both the themes of covenanting and electing could never in themselves lead to a position of Christian isolationism. Both point to an implicit relationship between the God of the old Israel and the new Israel and all peoples, and a longing and desire of that God to draw all into a relationship of kinship with himself. Any special relationship with a chosen people is for the purpose of leading all to one God. It is within this context that we must set relations with those of other faiths. There can be no room for superiority or pride, only for wonder and thanksgiving that we are called, marked, for service to others: to that pattern of service exemplified in the Isaianic Servant and perfected in Jesus Christ.

17

(iv)   The Incarnate God

38.   In the New Testament the story and interpretations of the life and death of Jesus of Nazareth are inextricably bound together. Mark begins his gospel leaving us in no doubt: 'The beginning of the gospel of Jesus Christ, the Son of God...'. And as we read his gospel that which is hidden becomes more and more obvious until the centurion witnessing the cruci-fixion confesses: 'Truly this man was the Son of God'. The resurrection and ascension set the seal on this claim. Paul and other New Testament writers struggle to explain this mystery of God entering human history. They use their contemporary categories to express the divinity of Jesus and his pre-existence. They talk of Jesus as the divine Wisdom of God and the Word of God, echoing thoughts from both the Old Testament and Greek philosophy.

39.   Following on such trajectories coming from Scripture, one tradition in the Early Fathers continued the exploration of the significance of Jesus and of his life and death. It develops the thought of the prologue to John's Gospel identifying Jesus as the divine, pre-existent Logos, agent in creation, who had manifested himself in various forms to Abraham, Isaac and Moses. In the second century Justin Martyr says that it was that same Logos who had been active in all, imparting to them whatever good-ness and knowledge they possessed. The idea in Justin's mind seems to have been that the presence of the Logos in Jesus Christ is to be under-stood as similar to a universal presence, though much greater in degree. Justin himself never developed the idea, leaving the presence of the Word in others in all ages itself unexplained. Nearer our own day Archbishop William Temple took up this exploration. In talking about the divine act in the incarnation he says that the incarnation does not require that God the Son should be active only in Jesus of Nazareth during the incarnation:

> '"The Light that lightens every man" did not cease to do so when he shone in full brilliance in one human life. Jesus did not control affairs in Mars, or in China. But God the Son, who is the Word of God by whom, as agent, all things come to be apart from whom no single thing has come to be, without ceasing His creative and sustaining work, added this to it, that He became flesh and dwelt as in a tabernacle among us, so that as in the old Tabernacle there dwelt the cloud of the Divine glory, so in Him we saw a glory that shone through Him but found in Him its perfect and unique expression - "Glory as of the Only Begotten Son from a Father".'[15]

40.   The development of Logos theology has implications for under-standing God's activity in the world and is therefore important for any assessment of Christian relations with other faiths. While Logos theology understands the unique expression of God as being in Jesus Christ (there can be no surrendering of that belief), at the same time it takes seriously other manifestations of the Logos in other places and at other times. This

suggests that in relations with those of other faiths Christians have to hold to that unique self-expressive activity of God in Jesus Christ, safeguarded and passed down within the Christian Church. But equally Christians need to be open to recognise and respond to all manifestations of the Logos. The decisive revelation of God in Jesus has to be safeguarded for that is the canon by which we are enabled to recognise all other manifestations. Furthermore in the encountering of those other revelations, new depths are discovered in that fullest revelation of God in Jesus Christ. Such reflection on the mystery of the person of Jesus in the Bible and Tradition points in the direction of an inclusivism in relation to those of other faiths, but with an unswerving loyalty to Jesus Christ.

41.   The Incarnation is suggestive in other ways. The pattern of the Incarnation is of God surrendering himself. In the Gospel stories he lives a life of openness to others. And as he opens himself to embrace all, he risks and becomes vulnerable embracing the way of suffering, even when it leads to death. The Incarnation is the sign of the God who does not stand over against but who identifies with all humanity, even the outsider and the sinner. Here is a pattern of relating to others so revolutionary that it is hard to grasp. But here is the pattern for Christian discipleship involving openness to others, the acceptance of vulnerability and of pain. It is this God who liberated through self-giving, whose great strength was proved paradoxically only in weakness that is the God whom Christians have to testify to in what they say and how they act in dialogue. To take this seriously is to accept both a pattern for dialogue and also the willingness to face those pains and transformations that will surely accompany it.

42.   As the New Testament writers began to reflect on what had happened in that life of apparent failure and defeat and as the Early Fathers picked up those biblical clues, in the life, death and resurrection of Jesus, they affirmed that these events had made a radical difference to life and not only to their individual lives, but to all life for all time. The Incarnation provided not only a pattern of discipleship, but in a way they knew, but could hardly explain, an objective difference for all creation. Whether that was described in sacrificial terms or in the language of 'Christus Victor', they were in no doubt about this once for all event which lifts all creation towards perfect union with God and leads all towards re-capitulation in Christ. No inter-faith dialogue can surrender this 'jealousy' of Christian belief and remain faithful to the essentials of Christianity.[16]

(v) God as Spirit

43.   We have seen that there is abundant biblical evidence to suggest that God is active in all nations amongst all peoples. What the writers of the Old Testament could only describe as the hand of God, the breath of God, the word of God, the Early Church came to understand from their reading and interpretation of the Scriptures and their own experience as the person of the Holy Spirit, the third person of the Trinity. The inner relation of the persons of the Trinity, that of mutual indwelling, and the separate spheres of activity of the divine persons of the Trinity, were the subjects of much discussion and controversy. Orthodox tradition talks of the 'economy of the Holy Spirit' distinct from that of the first or second persons of the Trinity. This enabled them to develop a strong theology of the Spirit's presence everywhere, filling everything, by virtue of an economy distinct from that of the Son. Irenaeus calls the Word and the Spirit the two hands of the Father. The West, on the other hand, with the adoption of the Filioque clause in the Nicene Creed pointed in another direction in which the advent of the Spirit in the world was dependent upon the Son. The Holy Spirit in the world tended to be thought of as subordinate to the Son and as a function of the Word.

44.   The present debate between Eastern and Western churches over the place of the Filioque clause in the Nicene Creed has some relevance for the inter-faith discussion. It is sometimes said by Eastern Christians that the Filioque tends to subordinate the Spirit to the Son in such a way that the Spirit's activity is closely tied to the institution which witnesses to the Son, rather than being seen as the agency which realizes in each and every person, according to their capacity, the new humanity perfectly manifest in the Son's incarnate life. Thus for many modern Orthodox writers, the 'economy' or dispensation of the Spirit is not simply a guarantee that the Christian Church or the Christian Scriptures carry the direct authority of the Word Incarnate; it is whatever is now driving us and challenging us and nurturing us into a lived Christlikeness. The Spirit's witness is fundamentally the fact of human lives now lived under the transfiguring sign of Cross and Resurrection; it is the showing of Christ as humanly contemporary. In principle the 'dispensations' of Son and Spirit are harmonious and complementary, neither making sense without the other; in practice, a certain tension is observable between form and realized content, the institutional and the charismatic.

45.   Whatever the justice of Orthodox strictures upon the alleged results of the Filioque, there is no denying that this vision of tension and complementarity between the historically visible, 'named', determinate presence and memory of God the Son and the more unpredictable, culturally and historically indeterminate witness of the Spirit provides a

possibly fruitful vehicle for a 'theology of religions'. What the Spirit does is never independent of the human and divine truth decisively shown in Jesus crucified and risen. The Spirit (as in John 16, for example) has nothing to give but Christ, and creates nothing that is not Christ's. The Spirit forms in us that intimacy with the Father which is the all-determining reality of Jesus' life and death. But there is no reason to conclude that the Spirit is impotent except where Jesus is named. Indeed, insofar as an imperfectly converted Church always hides or distorts Jesus as well as revealing him, it would be a curious diminution of God's freedom to say that the Spirit of Christ's truth cannot be shed abroad at all in the non-Christian world because of the sins of the Church. And although God is free to act beyond the visible Church, he is not free to be anything other than what he is, Father, Son, Spirit; so that if he speaks and acts in other religious cultures, he gives himself as he gives to us, as Father, in Spirit, manifest in Christlike form. If that form is fully explicit only to Christians, this means that to them is given the joy and the responsibility of recognition and proclamation as the Spirit uncovers to them in other faiths and cultures the deepest truth of their own Christian and human being, and works to convert them more fully to what they already experience. So the Spirit in us can communicate the focal historical concreteness of the work of God as Son, while the Spirit beyond the Church communicates to us the present human actuality of God as Son in ever more diverse and challenging forms and faces.

(vi)   The Saving and Judging God

46.   These reflections upon the central truths of Christianity, the Triune God, Creator, Redeemer and Sustainer, lead us to take serious account of the revelation of God in other religious traditions and cultures. At the same time it is clear that there can be no surrendering of the decisiveness of the Christ event. We turn now to another significant biblical pointer, important for any understanding of inter-faith relations, the saving and judging God. Here we encounter evidence which is difficult to assess. Different biblical strands seem to point in different directions. Some Christians, ignoring the complexity, have tended to use certain texts as discussion-stoppers, ways of blocking all debate about God's purposes with those of other faiths, and even the avoidance of relationships with them.

47.   There are many aspects of salvation developed and explored within the Bible. Both Old and New Testaments have numerous instances of salvation as understood in material and concrete ways: deliverance from disease, restoration of life, security from demonic attacks, the blessings of wealth and this-worldly happiness for individuals, and on the national

level, the victory and restoration of the kingdom of Israel in the land of Palestine. Such immediate and tangible acts of deliverance are all understood as salvation. But the Old Testament and the inter-testamental literature in particular move towards the concept of salvation as a future, eschatological event, the cessation of the afflictions and trials of this life and the dawning of a new age. This is a powerful theme of apocalyptic literature and of the ideas circulating during the first century, forming an important context for the development of thought in the New Testament. Although in the New Testament salvation is here and now with 'the breaking in of the kingdom' into this age, 'the consummation of the kingdom' belongs to the future beyond the final day of judgement. This notion of an other-worldly state of salvation complete only after death became normative for Christian ideas of salvation very early on in the history of the Church. Salvation was understood as deliverance, through the work of Christ, from sin, condemnation, perdition, death and the wrath of God. The form of this present world was passing and would pass away, but some would be saved in the day of the Lord Jesus. When salvation was understood in this way people began to speculate on who would and who would not be saved, in spite of Paul's warning to 'pass no premature judgement' (I Cor. 4.5).

48.   The formulation 'outside the Church, no salvation' has its roots at least as early as Cyprian in the middle of the third century. Indeed Catholic Christianity went on to affirm at the Council of Florence in the fifteenth century that:

> 'The Holy Roman Church firmly believes, professes and proclaims that none of those who are outside the Catholic Church - not only pagans, but Jews also, heretics and schismatics - can have part in eternal life, but will go into eternal fire, 'which was prepared for the devil and his angels', unless they are gathered into that Church before the end of life.'[17]

The Reformation tradition stemming from Luther and Calvin puts its emphasis elsewhere than upon membership of the visible Church but it is equally exclusive in its interpretation of the final destiny of the non-Christian, for 'apart from Jesus there is nothing except mere idolatry...', 'for whatever is outside faith (*extra fidem*) is idolatry'.[18] Such conceptions underlay the vivid sense of the lostness of the heathen that motivated the nineteenth century missionary movement as for example in Hudson Taylor: '... and every day tens of thousands were passing away to Christ-less graves. Perishing China so filled my heart and mind that there was no rest by day, and little sleep by night until my health broke down'. This sentiment lives on in many missionary hymns still sung today.[19] Moving nearer our own time, the Lausanne Covenant, 1974, can also be taken to point in this direction.[20] Such powerful statements of a doctrine of exclusion from salvation are taken by some to point in the direction of only the most distant of relations with those of other faiths.

49. Two biblical texts in particular have been quoted and indeed still are quoted to support such a view of exclusion from salvation of all who are not Christians. In Acts 4.12 Peter is represented as saying of Jesus:

> 'And there is salvation in no one else, for there is no other name under heaven given among men by which we must be saved.'

We suggested earlier that no biblical texts ought to be quoted against, or indeed in support of, any theory, without a consideration of its immediate context. This text like any other has to be explored in the context of the story in Acts chapters 3 and 4. A lame man is healed within the temple precincts. The healing is in the name of Jesus Christ of Nazareth. The miracle arouses great excitement so that a large crowd gathers and Peter preaches to them. As a result of the healing and preaching Peter and John are arrested and placed on trial before the Temple authorities. Peter is asked the question, 'By what power or by what name did you do this?' The answer is given in relation to the healing and the answer includes the witnessing to the name of Jesus Christ of Nazareth. The story is one of the series concerning wonder-workers and the use of 'the name'. Accordingly the story is about healing and the authority by which this takes place.

50. In the verse so often quoted to uphold an exclusivist view of Christianity it needs to be recognised that the word for 'saved' and also 'salvation' is that word which three verses earlier is translated as 'cured'. The word has a wide connotation of meanings ranging from 'healing', 'wholeness' to 'salvation'. The messianic quotation in verse 11, taken from Psalm 118, shows that in Peter's mind Jesus is indeed much more than simply a healer, a worker of miracles. Peter knows that Jesus is the one through whom God has chosen to restore the wholeness of creation. Nevertheless the immediate issue is by what power the cripple has been made well. His reply is not intended to deny the existence of other healings (compare the Beelzebub controversy in Matthew 12.22-30), but to claim that all healing, all making whole, belong to Jesus. It is going beyond the text to interpret it as a statement about other faiths. The context, as Bishop John Robinson emphasises, is not one of comparative religion.[21]

51. A similar approach can be taken with another passage often taken out of context to uphold a rigidly exclusivist view, John 14.6.

> 'Jesus said to him, "I am the way, and the truth, and the life; no-one comes to the Father, but by me".'

Taken like this out of context there can be little doubt that it appears to support such a view. But again the text ought to be interpreted only within the development of thought in the discourse as a whole and then set within a wider framework of biblical thought. The context is that of

Thomas' question about how the disciples can know where Jesus is going, and therefore how they can know the way. The answer is that Jesus is going to the Father, and since they know him they have no need to demand as Philip did, 'Show us the Father': indeed to have seen Jesus was to have seen the Father. John is here trying to assure the disciples that to have seen Jesus is indeed to have seen nothing less than God, for God is perfectly reflected in Jesus, as indeed the prologue to this gospel is at pains to show. Again, in the words of John Robinson, 'the Father is perfectly reflected in him, he is God, all through'. There is no suggestion in the context that Jesus is claiming to be 'the whole of God', that outside him there is no truth or life to be found. The main thrust is that in him truth and life are to be found, that same truth and life which belong to the Father. There is therefore no cause for fear. When we read the text in this way there is no need to suppose that it is claiming that apart from Jesus there is neither truth nor life. That is indeed too limiting an interpretation to fit in with the rest of John's Gospel.

52.   It is then possible to read these hard sayings as having a different connotation for inter-faith relations. However, we would not want to press that ours is the only interpretation, nor to obscure the fact that a very powerful and influential exclusivism did indeed emerge in the early centuries which has persisted as one strand in Christianity and still has its adherents.

53.   There are, however, strands within the Bible, developed in Christian theology, which point clearly towards an inclusive understanding of salvific work. In the Gospel of Luke Jesus himself is pictured as selecting two events of the Old Testament to make just such a point: Elijah's protecting of the widow at Sarepta and Elisha's healing of Naaman the Syrian. Again, this message is acted out dramatically in Jesus' healing of the Syro-Phoenician woman and his words to her. When the woman protests that even children and dogs share the same diet, she shows that Jesus is making a false distinction between Jew and Gentile. Jesus marvellously accepts the argument, and confirms her view. He learns from her, his own boundaries are being enlarged, his attitudes shifted by a woman, a voteless pagan, who for his disciples was just a nuisance. In spite of the fact that Jesus was committed first of all to his own people and only released fully in a universal dimension at Pentecost, the signs of such a dimension are clearly there in his own lifetime.

54.   Perhaps the most powerful pointer to the inclusiveness of God's saving activity is the story of the conversion of Cornelius, more tellingly renamed, the conversion of Peter. The length and detail of the story confirms its importance for the early Christian community's understanding of its identity (Acts 10 and 11). Guided by the Spirit the Church was

led to acknowledge the lack of partiality of God and his concern for the Gentiles. This is the point of the story.

55.   Equally the story shows how hard it was even for Peter to take hold of the notion of the impartiality of God. Statements made in the story are important clues for a Christian understanding of the status before God of those who are not Christians in our own day. Cornelius is described in Acts 10.2 as a 'devout man' (*eusebes,* a word used in the Septuagint to translate the Hebrew words for just, loyal to God, and noble). Furthermore, Cornelius 'fears God', words which echo that reverential fear which is the beginning of wisdom. He gives alms to the people and prays constantly. He is *dikaios,* 'good' (NEB) as indeed were Abraham and Noah in Genesis. What is more, the author reports Peter as acknowledging that Cornelius is one among those in every nation who similarly fear God and do right.

56.   Clearly the affirmation in this story is that God is indeed no respecter of persons. The challenge is to the ethnocentricity of the first Jerusalem Church and to Christian neo-Judaism. Hence the categorical affirmation, this man is *dektos,* acceptable to God, as were 'the creatures of every kind' that Peter saw in his vision on the rooftop. It was not for him to decide whom God would or would not accept. Cornelius' prayers are heard, his alms remembered before God, they ascend as memorials before God. The language used by the author of Acts as he interprets for us the amazing event of Cornelius' conversion is thoroughly dependent on the Septuagint. In particular the passage echoes one of the themes of the book of Ecclesiasticus (Ben Sirach) which shows how in one strand of Jewish thought, the 'good man' who lived outside the covenant was viewed. Those who live according to Torah, even though they do not belong to the nation of those who possess the law, are illuminated by the Logos and their conscience bears their witness. They even belong within the 'eternal covenant' of which Ben Sirach speaks.[22]

57.   The story of Peter and Cornelius testifies to one theme constant in Christian tradition down to our own time. It is already explicit in Justin in the second century.

> 'It is our belief that those men who strive to do the good which is enjoined on us have a share in God; according to our traditional belief they will by God's grace share his dwelling. And it is our conviction that this holds good in principle for all men. Christ is the divine Word in whom the whole human race share, and those who live according to the light of their knowledge are Christians, even if they are considered as being godless.'[23]

And in our own day the same theme was echoed in the powerful statements of the Second Vatican Council. In the document on the Dogmatic Constitution on the Church (*Lumen Gentium*):

'Those who, through no fault of their own, do not know the Gospel of Christ or his Church, but who nevertheless seek God with a sincere heart, and, moved by grace, try in their actions to do his will as they know it through the dictates of their conscience - those too may achieve eternal salvation ... Whatever good or truth is found amongst them is considered by the Church to be a preparation for the Gospel and given by him who enlightens all men that they may at length have life.'[24]

This should not be taken to imply that we may declare who has attained everlasting salvation or who has not; nor that the Church's vocation to mission is the less compelling.

58.   Nevertheless the story in Acts makes it plain that through his encounter with Peter Cornelius received something more, namely the gift of baptism, the conforming into the life, death and resurrection of Christ and 'repentance unto life' (Acts 11.8). In his account of the story to the Jerusalem church Peter told how the angel had said to Cornelius: '"Send to Joppa and bring Simon called Peter; he will declare to you a message by which you will be saved, you and all your household".' Through baptism Cornelius and his household were incorporated within the community of the Church in its earthly manifestation. We may recognise the grace of God at work outside the confines of the Church leading to salvation, and yet at the same time this story does not allow us to see baptism into the Body of Christ as irrelevant or at most an optional extra.

59.   There is a further significant point for us in the Cornelius story. The encounter not only brings a change in Cornelius and his household but in Peter too. Through Cornelius' style of life, through his righteousness which is acceptable to God, Peter himself learns something of the nature and being of God. Peter's own horizons are enlarged. This is a possibility for all who engage in inter-faith situations, if they can show the same openness and willingness to be led by the Spirit as Peter showed in his relations with Cornelius.

60.   The Bible does not offer a comprehensive or definitive solution on the question of the relation of Christians to those of other faiths in the twentieth century. Indeed the situation in which the Bible was formed was so different from our own that we could hardly expect to find in it a blueprint for contemporary relationships. Nevertheless it does provide sufficient and significant pointers for Christians in their search for a theology of inter-faith dialogue.

61.   The Triune God is a God who moved in creation into a relationship with all that is created; who as the Word, is incarnate in Jesus and yet encountered in other places; and who as Holy Spirit, present in the Church and in the lives of baptised Christians, is also active among those of other faiths and cultures. It is the same God whose saving grace is at work outside the Church as well as within it. These powerful biblical pointers must inform a Christian understanding of our relations with those of other faiths. What would be contrary to the biblical witness would be the abandonment of a defining loyalty to Jesus Christ as the one in whom God was reconciling the whole world to himself and any proposal that this message of reconciliation through Christ need no longer be offered to those of other faiths. The inclusive invitation of God goes now, as always, with the demand for an exclusive loyalty to his Anointed. It is such biblical pointers which have to be brought to bear on the experience of Christians in the changed context of Britain in the nineteen eighties. This interplay of Scripture, Tradition and experience provides the beginnings of a theology for inter-faith relations, and provides a basis for looking again at the four guidelines on dialogue accepted by the General Synod in 1981:

1. dialogue begins when people meet each other
2. dialogue depends upon mutual understanding and mutual trust
3. dialogue makes it possible to share in service to the community
4. dialogue becomes the medium of authentic witness.

62.   Dialogue Begins when People Meet each Other

'It began the day we moved in. As the removal van drew up, children and adults appeared as if from nowhere and helped to carry furniture and fittings into our new home. And we had met none of them previously. Afterwards we went round to express our thanks. Their welcome was overwhelming, and soon we were talking like old friends; even our lack of Urdu and their limited English only added to the fun. Since then we have sampled one another's traditional foods, exchanged gifts, shared in parties and discussed the similarities and differences we'd noticed about our separate faiths.'

'People of other faiths do not live in books but down our streets!' Because of the changed context in Britain today dialogue between Christianity and other faiths can no longer be an impersonal exchange between theoretical systems left to a few theologians. Dialogue is a way of life, a personal encounter in community. Where families meet as neighbours, where children play together and where men and women work side by side or stand together in the unemployment queue, dialogue is related to the whole of life and becomes a style of 'living-in-relationship.'[25]

63.   Dialogue as a personal encounter in community is not encouraged by Christians on the grounds of the expediency of peaceful co-existence. It is rather the outworking of those theological pointers examined above, and springs from an interest in others for their own sake and for God's sake and not from any motive to proselytise. What impels us to dialogue is the belief that we are all created in the image of God, share a common humanity and all live in the presence of God. It is the response to the command 'to love our neighbours as ourselves'. God is amongst them as amongst us, we are not the sole heirs to truth and divine knowledge. Further, to enter willingly into relations with people of other faiths is to honour the variety of God's creation, his love and desire for all.

64.   But the opportunities for this new style of dialogue-in-living are sadly all too often rejected. It is more comfortable to cling to those with whom we recognise an identity on the basis of shared religious belief and cultural background. Our deeply rooted sense of identity with some communities and alienation from others is a complex matter, never completely understood, but it remains a powerful reality for each one of us and we more readily cut ourselves off from those who are different. If Christians, who in Britain are in the majority, find it hard to come out of their isolation, how much harder it is for those in minority groups living in very different cultural contexts. The following story illustrates both the problems of the new situation in Britain and the possibility of creativity when Christians take a lead.

65.   'On one occasion I was approached as the Bishop's adviser in community relations by a parish priest to come and do something about the growing hostility among his congregation towards the Pakistanis who had moved and were still moving into the area. The neighbourhood was a "run-down suburb" of a Yorkshire woollen town. Whole streets were being taken over and the local schools were sprinkled with growing numbers of brown faces. Verbal abuse and petty assaults at bus stops were on the increase. The gulf between the two communities could hardly have been any wider. Together with the vicar we worked out a plan of campaign to try and reverse the situation. He published a series of short articles in his parish magazine on the basics of Islam in preparation for a parish conference on Sunday afternoon on Christian mission to Muslims in the neighbourhood. It was attended by eleven elderly ladies who had come more out of loyalty to the vicar than out

of interest in the subject. I brought with me a Yorkshire lady - one like themselves - from a neighbouring town who with her family had stayed on in an area which was being taken over by the Indian Muslim community. She spoke to them about her experiences of living among them, of the friendships she had made and what she had discovered about their family life and customs. She so awakened their interest that they wanted to hear more about the religion of Islam.

'Some months later two English-speaking Muslim leaders came to address a large meeting made up of members of two local churches and they held them spellbound. Spontaneously at the end the Muslim speakers with some Muslim students in the audience agreed to say their *ischa* prayer in our explanation of *wuzu,* the rite of ablutions. The prolonged silence which followed their prayer indicated that somehow we Christians had been caught up in that worship; its God-centredness and the unselfconscious concentration of the worshippers touched a deep chord in us. For the majority if not for all of us it was the first time that we had experienced Muslim worship. On the spiritual level the gulf between east and west had been bridged.

'From this event a real friendship began to grow between the vicar and the local imam. They began to call on each other and when racial incidents occurred in the school they both took a hand in restoring calm by visiting the school together. To create and strengthen bonds of mutual respect between their two communities they organised a party for children and parents in the church hall with a buffet of English and Asian foods. Parishioners found themselves shaking hands with Pakistani men (the women of course were absent) about whom they recently had been expressing hostile opinions. The vicar with the imam's approval began visiting Pakistani homes where invariably he found a warm welcome and on occasions he was even asked to pray for God's blessing on the family where there was any sickness.

'The key to that whole development of relationships between the two communities lay with the open and positive attitudes on the part of both the vicar and the imam.'

66.   Dialogue Depends on Mutual Understanding and Mutual Trust

As those of different faiths grow in confidence and learn to trust each other there is the opportunity for sustained conversation and exchange. This involves the willingness both to listen attentively to the other and the attempt to contribute sensitively our own view of things. In dialogue we listen and speak and search together, believing that each has something to communicate and that no one person, no single system is the depository of the whole truth.

67.   Listening in dialogue is not passive. As the dictionary definition suggests, to listen is to make an effort to hear! It demands a quality of

creative awareness of the other which means letting go of ourselves, not only hearing words spoken, but trying to understand what is being said from the perspective of the speaker. And it means attempting to interpret the significance of the silences of the partner. Here the problem of language, of translating terms from one conceptual framework to another, makes demands upon both those who speak and those who listen. When people of different faiths are in dialogue they need to be aware of the structures and nuances of language, thought and imagery that belong to different religious traditions. For example, Jesus in Christianity has a quite different role to that of Muhammad in Islam or Gotama in Buddhism. Similarly the significance of, and approach to, the scriptures will be distinctive, the Bible occupying a different role for Christians than the Qur'an does for Muslims. These broad differences creep into the accepted symbols of religion too. The concept of God as Father, freely encouraged by Christians, would be unacceptable to most Muslims, for it would not provide the best model of God in their view. The unravelling of such interwoven skeins is part of dialogue, a process which can only be achieved by patience and understanding.

The importance of learning to share in another religious tradition's views can be illustrated by a question in a GCE paper where the candidate was invited to comment on the importance of Moses for Judaism as 'a Saviour and Redeemer of Israel', concepts which would be unacceptable to the Jew regarding Moses. The Christian terminology makes assumptions about the centrality and activity of Moses in the Jewish religion that do not fit the general Jewish view.

68.   Listening in inter-faith dialogue demands that we are prepared to grapple with the religious and cultural systems through which others express their faith and that we seek to avoid interpreting what they are saying in terms of concepts and words in our Christian system.

69.   If listening in dialogue makes its demands, so too does speaking. Contributing means understanding with as much clarity as possible our own inheritance and cultures, it means living more faithfully in the tradition we seek to explain and offer. For Christians commitment to inter-faith dialogue has to go hand in hand with a deeper commitment to the Christian tradition. This comes from living within the worshipping community and engaging with the central truths of Christianity in eucharistic celebration. It is here we encounter, at the deepest level, that which is unique and from which we are sent out in the power of the Spirit renewed for dialogue.

70.   This dialectical process in dialogue, this demanding pattern of listening attentively as well as contributing sensitively is a pattern discernible in the biblical witness. We see it in the ministry of Jesus as he enters into

dialogue with the Jewish leaders of his own day. But it is there also in the listening and interpreting that is the rhythm behind the biblical process of revelation.

71. Those Christians who have already listened most carefully in interfaith dialogue acknowledge the richness of insight to be discovered in other faiths. They have found their own perceptions of God echoed, and have been led to new understandings of what is cradled in the Christian tradition. In such dialogue we too may expect to have our view of God illuminated by the insights, sensitivities and religious experiences of members of other faiths. This must be so from what we have understood from the Bible of the work of God the Creator, the Logos and the Spirit.

72. But equally a part of that mutual understanding and trust which characterises dialogue involves acknowledging that there will be, on both sides, beliefs and positions that cannot be surrendered. Dialogue can never be seen as an easy way of overlooking the essential differences leading to a form of syncretism. Both Norman Anderson and Stephen Neill have explored points of tension and disagreement between Christianity and other faiths. There are what have been called 'jealousies' that have to be protected. As we have certain beliefs that we have affirmed we may not surrender, so also those of other religions have beliefs they will not surrender and which cannot be reconciled with ours. There are contradictions in our religious positions. Dialogue, if it follows the incarnational pattern, will not cease upon the recognition that each side believes the deepest insight to be on its side. In engaging with those of other faiths we must accept that no dialogue is possible unless we are actually prepared to acknowledge the magnitude of our differences. In 1977, the Bishop of Winchester pleaded with those who wish to make all intractable convictions relative and level them down for the sake of a quick reconciliation, 'Leave us at least our capacity for categorical assertions, for that is what we have in common'.[26]

73. **Dialogue Makes it Possible to Share in Service to the Community**

This kind of meeting and exploration of each other's positions makes it possible to share in serving the community. An important element in the Christian vocation is the commitment to work for the establishment of God's Kingdom on earth; a commitment to struggle against all forms of brokenness in human community, to break down barriers of race, sex, and class and to overthrow all unjust social structures. There is the Christian commitment to serve the community in education, health care and the social services, to struggle against the unequal distribution of the world's resources, and to seek to understand the inter-connection of peace and justice. The motives for such action are there in the Gospel: Jesus, the servant, leaves to his church the role of servant; Jesus, the prophet, delegates to his church the role of speaking out for those who have no-one to speak for them: he who inaugurates the Kingdom leaves to his church the responsibility of labouring for a community which has the marks of heaven about it. In all of this Christians must join wherever they can in common cause with all who seek to serve the human community.

74. Although we may be able to seek common cause in the service of our fellows for a kingdom on earth we need to recognise that there will often be differences in emphasis which will lead to separate action. The values we seek to enshrine in the structures of society may well differ as we discover differences in our understanding of the nature of God, and what we perceive of that nature will determine the values we seek to enshrine. Similarly, different views on human nature may lead to different patterns of living. A very obvious example of this is the difference in the Christian and Muslim understanding of the relation of the sexes. For Muslims the significance of single-sex schooling of children over the age of eleven is crucial, it is an issue which cannot be divorced from the total Muslim view of women, marriage and inter-sex relations. The problem is bound up in the faith, and cannot be conveniently treated as a separate issue. The coherence of faith systems needs to be understood and respected. Christians in seeking for the wholeness of society must not neglect the different outlooks and beliefs of those of other faiths even when they challenge and affront their own beliefs.

75. Nevertheless it is in seeking to serve our fellow human beings that the barriers of mistrust and misunderstanding can be removed. And no Christian can evade the Gospel demands for commitment to the establishment of God's Kingdom of justice and peace.

76. Dialogue Becomes the Medium of Authentic Witness

A relationship of dialogue based upon mutual understanding and mutual trust which issues in shared service to the community is for the Christian an opportunity for authentic witness: that is, witness to what God has done in Jesus in reconciling the world to himself. We cannot deny that which we believe to be true, which we receive in Scripture and Tradition within the community of the Church. But neither can authentic witness be given without proper respect for the other person and their right to be free. They must be given the right to define themselves without manipulation or coercion. There can be no place for the one-sided and harsh ways of proselytism for that would be to violate the rights of every human being to freedom. Indeed the pattern of the Incarnation itself shows us God in Jesus respecting his creatures and allowing them to respond or to reject him.

77. To enter such a relationship, respecting the freedom of others to define themselves, and opening ourselves to respond, means accepting vulnerability and taking risks. It means risking that we will be changed in the experience for we may be called to acknowledge the implications for our own faith of the spiritual experiences, sensitivities and traditions of those of other faiths. We may be called to acknowledge the light shining there that reveals to us a deeper and truer understanding of the Christ to whom we would bear authentic witness. It may well be that the questions and the witness of those of other faiths may renew our own understandings, judge that which is unauthentic in our own witness, and refine and balance the witness we seek to make.

78. In dialogue authentic witness is not only given in the words we speak but in the manner and bearing of the life we live. Human frailty and sin mean that Christians have always to struggle towards consistency between the message they proclaim and the image they present in life. To confess Jesus the Crucified as Lord, the one who wins our freedom and life, is denied when we use powers of coercion over others; to confess the Spirit at work outside the Church as well as within, is denied when we refuse to listen attentively to others. In the same way to talk of God as One God who desires the unity of human community, and to proclaim this as divided Christians is to contradict the authenticity of that message.

79. Inevitably people will ask what dialogue bearing these marks of openness and vulnerability has to do with the mission of the Church. Christians may never surrender a commitment to mission though the monologue is a style which should be relegated to the colonial past. Dialogue that bears authentic witness to Jesus Christ is a valid part of the Church's multi-faceted task of mission. Mission and dialogue do belong together. This realisation is not new. We see it in the Church's mission in the norms given by St. Francis of Assisi to the friars who desired to go among Muslims. He describes to them a way which would not raise arguments or disputes, in which they should be subject to every creature for the love of God and still confess themselves to be Christians. Only then, when they perceive it pleasing to God, should they announce the Word of God. Similarly, nearer our own day the experience of Charles de Foucauld shows the dialogical way of mission, where mission is exercised in the Islamic world through the sharing of life with those of another faith in a humble and silent attitude of union with God and in service to the poor. The same can be found nearer our own day in the ministries of such men as Temple Gairdner and Bishop Kenneth Cragg, people deeply respected by Muslims for their scholarship in Islam and for their Christian faith, who have pioneered as missionaries the way of dialogue.

80.   And so we carry our mission into dialogue as people who speak from faith to faith. All genuine dialogue has a dimension of mission. For some this will imply the eventual possibility that all will be converted to Christ; for others it will be sufficient that each participant in dialogue has fully and fairly borne witness to their faith so that each understands more about the commitment of the other. Mission in the context of dialogue, without coercion, acknowledging fully the integrity of the other above all, creates the context in which the Holy Spirit can work. It is the Holy Spirit, the principal agent for mission, who alone can convert. Women and men are instruments of and co-workers with the Triune God.

FINAL REFLECTIONS

81. The journey through unfamiliar territory, which inter-faith dialogue is for most of us, raises many of the major themes of Christian doctrine. We for our part have been excited by the way in which the debate and controversies of past ages have taken on a freshness and a new relevance. We have been forced to look again at what it is we believe and by listening to one another have begun to sense that the Spirit is leading us into new perceptions.

82. Those who have already begun the journey into such unfamiliar territory have reminded us that theology is always provisional. It is out of our experience in dialogue with our Tradition, under the power of the Holy Spirit, that our theology flows. We are given to the Spirit who is with us and who goes before us.

83. Those who would journey with us into the unfamiliar territory must learn to accept the stance of vulnerability which dialogue brings with it. Our discipleship is revealed for what it is, as our understanding and faith are put to the test. We discover that it is out of weakness and not strength that we make our witness and our appeal.

84. As more Christians enter into dialogue with those of other faiths we shall be able to discern more clearly what the Spirit is saying to the churches. For our part we have found a consensus. It can be described as being inclusivist with an exclusivist loyalty to Jesus Christ. We expect that God will speak to us through the sensitivities and experiences of devout men and women of other faiths. We expect our own faith to be challenged, refined and at times judged, but we are firm in our loyalty to the revelation of God in and through the life, death and resurrection of Jesus of Nazareth. What we have to offer is only a beginning. We ask understanding, encouragement and prayer for those whom God has called to a particular ministry of dialogue with those of other faiths.

85. We believe with Bishop David Brown, who began this journey with us, that:

> '...Christ will provide the link by which the different religions will be brought into a deep and mutually enriching relationship with each other ... The apostle Paul declares his hope that God would one day "put his hidden purpose into effect and bring the universe, all in heaven and on earth, into a unity in Christ", and, in his great vision, John saw the universal city lit by the glory of God in and through Christ. There is much theological work to be done and many generations of dialogue before such a hope can ever come to fruition; but the task is a priority to which the churches must now give their attention!'[27]

FOOTNOTES TO THE REPORT

[1] *Relations with People of Other Faiths; Guidelines for Dialogue in Britain,* Revised Edition, 1983, British Council of Churches.

[2] Report of Proceedings of General Synod, Vol. 12, No. 3, 1981.

[3] Report of Proceedings of General Synod, Vol. 14, No. 1, 1983.

[4] *School Worship:* a Discussion Paper, CIO Publishing, 1984. *Our Ministry and Other Faiths,* CIO Publishing, 1984. *Can We Pray Together?,* BCC, 1983.

[5] *Gathered for Life,* WCC Publications, Geneva, 1984, p.31f.

[6] *Relations with People of Other Faiths,* cf. p.2, for community figures on the numbers of those of other faiths resident in Britain.

[7] The term 'pluralism' is used in different ways. Its use in this paragraph must be distinguished from its use, for example, to describe the pluralist state, theological pluralism, and pluralisms in relation to race and culture.

[8] J. Macquarrie, *Principles of Christian Theology,* Revised Edition, 1977.

[9] A. Barnard, *Tell us the Story,* BRF, 1980.
   T. G. A. Baker, *What is the New Testament?,* SCM, 1969.

[10] S. Mowinckel, *He that Cometh,* Oxford, 1956.
   A. R. Johnson, *Sacral Kingship in Ancient Israel,* Cardiff, 1967.
   J. H. Eaton, *Kingship in the Psalms,* Studies in Biblical Theology, No. 32, 1976.

[11] J. L. Mays, *Hosea,* SCM Press, 1969.

[12] G. von Rad, *Wisdom in Israel,* London, 1972.

[13] R. N. Whybray, *Wisdom in Proverbs,* Studies in Biblical Theology, No. 45, 1965.

[14] Edward Lohse, *The New Testament Environment,* SCM, 1974.

[15] William Temple, *Christus Veritas,* 1924, p.140.

[16] J. V. Taylor, *The Theological Basis of Inter-faith Dialogue,* 1979.

[17] Denziger/Schonmetzer, *Enchiridion Symbolorum,* Edition 29, Number 1324.

[18] Luther, *Weimar Collected Works,* Vol. 40, 2 page 111 and 40, 1 page 609.

[19] The heathen perish: day by day
   Thousands upon thousands pass away;
   O Christians to their rescue fly,
   Preach Jesus to them ere they die.   (J. Montgomery 1771-1854)

   O'er heathen lands afar
   Thick darkness broodeth yet;
   Arise, O morning star,
   Arise, and never set.   (L. Hensley 1824-1905)

[20] 'We recognise that all men have some knowledge of God through his general revelation in nature. But we deny that this can save, for men suppress the truth through their unrighteousness. We also reject as derogatory to Christ and the Gospel every kind of syncretism and dialogue that implies that God speaks equally through all religions and ideologies. Jesus Christ, being himself the only God-man, who gave himself as the only ransom for sinners, is the only mediator between God and man. There is no other name by which we must be saved. All men are

perishing because of sin, but God loves all men, not wishing that any should perish
but that all should repent. Yet those who reject Christ repudiate the joy of salvation and condemn themselves to eternal separation from God.'

Let the Earth Hear His Voice, ed. J. D. Douglas

[21] J. A. T. Robinson, *Truth is Two Eyed,* p.105 ff., SCM Press, London, 1979.

[22] Ecclesiasticus (Ben Sirach) 17: 1-2.

[23] 1 Apology 46: 1-4.

[24] Austin Flannery, OP (ed.), *Vatican Council II: The Conciliar and Post-Conciliar Documents,* Dominican Publications, Ireland, p.367 f.

[25] Peter Loveitt in *With People of Other Faiths in Britain.*

[26] J. V. Taylor, *The Theological Basis of Inter-faith Dialogue,* 1977.

[27] D. Brown, *All Their Splendour,* p.221, Fount Paperbacks, 1982.

EXTRACTS FROM 'BONDS OF AFFECTION'

Inter-Faith Relations were debated at the sixth meeting of the Anglican Consultative Council (ACC-6) held in Nigeria in 1984. We quote from its report *Bonds of Affection,* pp. 84-86.

Resolution 20 RELATIONS WITH ISLAM

Be it resolved that ACC-6:

(a) Recommends that our Communion seek direct contact with the Roman Catholic Church (the ACC with the Secretariat for Non-Christian Religions in Rome) and the World Council of Churches to explore the possibility of establishing joint international dialogue between Christians and the World Muslim Federation. Areas that could be examined would include ways in which the two communities can the better live together, the application of Sharia, mutual respect, etc.

(b) Recommends that a statement be made by the Archbishop of Canterbury, with other Church leaders as appropriate, when a serious situation occurs, such as the one in the Sudan. (The effect of this is to raise the issue to a higher profile as well as giving encouragement to people involved in the particular situation).

(c) Recommends that should an invitation come from the Church in Sudan, the Archbishop of Canterbury in conjunction with the Secretary General of ACC appoint a team from our Communion to make a visit to the Sudan.

(d) Recommends that all member churches be responsive to the special needs of the Church in Sudan, giving support in prayer, through visits and by all other means that are appropriate.

(e) Recommends to the Secretary General of ACC that the Secretary for Mission and Social Concerns be asked to take a special concern for this particular issue.

INTER-FAITH RELATIONS

The discussion of Christian-Muslim relations led us into the wider area of all inter-faith contacts between Christians and the other major faith communities in the world. A booklet prepared for the General Synod of the Church of England, *Towards a Theology for Inter-Faith Dialogue,* prompted a good deal of discussion.

This book views our relationships with other religions as important and attempts to state a theological support for such contact and dialogue. Three categories of response to other faiths are listed: exclusivism, which allows for very little, if any, dialogue; inclusivism, which allows for

38

dialogue within certain boundaries; and pluralism, which encourages open-ended dialogue. Christians can be found in all three of these categories and, indeed, some may find themselves moving from one position to another.

We thought the book needed a greater emphasis on the doctrine of redemption, and we questioned some of its biblical exegesis, as well as the selectivity of biblical texts. People from non-Western societies especially found the approach too academic and cerebral, and thus it was classified as largely irrelevant to them.

Our commitment, however, to developing inter-faith relationships is to be maintained. It is important for all God's creatures that differing faith communities live together in co-operation in the world. There is, in any event, not really an option to do otherwise for Christians who believe that all people are made in God's image and so are capable of revealing something of God. Moreover, Christians, in seeking to love their neighbours as themselves, realize that empathy and understanding are ways of both showing and developing that love.

Wherever possible, Christians are to witness to their faith by being in service to those in great need. This can be done on behalf of or in co-operation with those of other faiths along with efforts to change the conditions which cause poverty and injustice. In some situations this may be all that is possible. In one previous section we recognized that practical ways of co-operation may be all that can even be attempted between Christians and Muslims in many areas.

In other circumstances, however, Christians may find considerable benefits in telling of their faith to those of different religions and in turn hearing of their beliefs. Christians may differ with respect to what they expect they may learn of God from those of other religions, but all of us can have our love deepened and we may also learn better to clarify our own faith understandings. Always we may pray, too, that through us in such exchanges Jesus may speak to others.

Up vistaed hopes I sped;
And shot, precipitated,
Adown Titanic glooms of chasmed fears,
From those strong Feet that followed, followed after.
But with unhurrying chase,
And unperturbèd pace,
Deliberate speed, majestic instancy,
They beat - and a Voice beat
More instant than the Feet -
'All things betray thee, who betrayest Me.'

Francis Thompson
from 'The Hound of Heaven'

An old man was wandering around town
with a lamp in his hand saying,
'I am tired of hunters and beasts of prey,
I seek a man!'
I said to him, 'Such a one is not to be found,
we have sought him far.'
He said, 'That which is not to be found,
that is my desire!'

Jalaluddin Rumi from the Diwan-i-Shams-i-Tabriz

THAT WHICH IS NOT TO BE FOUND BUT WHICH FINDS US

Michael J. Nazir-Ali

Inter-faith dialogue often takes place in a context wider than the merely religious. It is not simply an exchange of information about each other's religious beliefs nor is it merely the swapping of accounts of religious experience. Both discussion about religious beliefs and the recounting of paradigmatic religious experience are important aspects of dialogue but they are not all of it. Inter-faith dialogue cannot be taken in isolation from the socio-political and economic conditions which exist in the society where such dialogue is being carried out. Religion, and in a plural situation the religion of the majority, tends to be a factor in the maintenance of the status quo and is indeed used to legitimize the oppression of minority and marginalized groups. In such a situation authentic inter-faith dialogue must not be merely the scholarly exchange of information about each other's religion, nor must it be simply a discussion group of the mystically inclined; it must bring to the fore sharp and uncomfortable questions about the role of religion in society and must set the 'prophetic' against the merely 'cultic'. Muslims, therefore, are entirely right when they, in the context of dialogue, raise the question of the legitimization of institutionalized racism, whether in South Africa or in the Middle East, in the name of the Bible. Again, it is not an exaggeration to suggest that Christianity's historical encounter with Hinduism posed a sharp challenge to the very basis on which traditional Hindu society was organized. This challenge became a significant factor in the reform and renewal of Hinduism in the nineteenth and twentieth centuries.[1] In the Indian context, moreover, as many Indian Christians have pointed out, Casteism and its religious justification must form an item on the agenda of Christian–Hindu dialogue today.[2] In the same way, as the present writer has noted elsewhere, in dialogue with Muslims the Christian will want to discuss what should be our common commitment to basic human rights; he will seek to discover in what ways the rights of women and other powerless groups are being protected within the house of Islam, and what Islam can contribute towards the growth of a consensus regarding basic social justice in our world.

All these aspects of Muslim–Christian dialogue are not extra to the agenda for inter-faith dialogue in this context but are at the centre, for they involve Muslim and Christian world-views, ideas on the nature of revelation, beliefs about divine ordering of society and many other matters central to both faith systems.[3]

It is extremely important in the Anglican context (and here I include in this context the United Churches, the Mar Thoma Syrian Church, the Philippine Independent Church and the Old Catholics. All those, in brief, who enjoy full communion with Canterbury) to recognise the historic nature of inter-faith encounter. In some provinces, it is true, inter-faith encounter has only just begun, but there are many others where it has been a fact of daily life for centuries. Anglicans in the Middle East, for example, have the vast resources of the ancient Churches there to draw upon in coming to a realistic *modus vivendi* with Islam. Such resources, of course, have to be critically used. For example, it may not be necessary to arrive at the same accommodations and the same compromises which were forced on the ancient Churches. Present world-concern for religious minorities, the presence of Muslim minorities in hitherto traditionally Christian countries and the Muslim insistence that they must be free in every context to practise Da'wah (or invitation to Islam) make today's situation rather different from yesterday's.

In our context, therefore, different models for Muslim–Christian co-existence and dialogue are both desirable and available. One such model, which sees the future Christian Church as possibly numerically small and politically powerless in the Middle East, argues that survival may depend upon not being seen as a threat to the major community and in establishing servant structures in the Church which allow it to be seen as a serving and therefore necessary community.[4] In other situations, such as the south-east Asian, other models, which allow Christians to strive more actively for social and political emancipation within a secular system, may be more appropriate.

Again, in the Indian subcontinent the centuries-long experience of the St Thomas Christians, their considerable integration into the Hindu social order and yet the maintenance of their distinctiveness, are surely worthy of study. The problem is that the Anglican theology of inter-faith dialogue has often in fact been British-specific.[5] Thus the comparative newness of a plural society in Great Britain has been emphasized and the pioneering nature of inter-faith dialogue in this context has been promoted. The specificity of the context, however, has led to a loss of historic consciousness regarding the issue. Such a loss, moreover, has been a loss for the British context as well, and accounts for the fact that in the British context of inter-faith dialogue little attention is paid to the views of Asian, African and Latin American Christians resident in Britain. An adequate historical perspective would most certainly prove helpful in furthering inter-faith dialogue in Britain today. The lack of historical consciousness has resulted, as has been pointed out, in insufficient account being taken of Churches and Christians in non-Western plural situations. Such situations are of different kinds:

(a) *Where Christians are a majority.* These situations are very rarely taken into account. Examples are the Philippines in Asia, Ethiopia and (say) Uganda in Africa. In the Philippines, for example, both the Roman

Catholic Church and the National Council of Churches have encouraged Christian–Muslim dialogue with a view to removal of prejudice, recognition of common citizenship and the development of mutual trust. I was told by Filipino NCC officials that *they* had campaigned successfully for the appointment of a cabinet minister to protect Muslim interests! In the Muslim majority island of Mindanao a Roman Catholic bishop has set the whole ministry of his prefecture in the context of Muslim–Christian dialogue. A great deal of prejudice and distrust remains, but what is being done deserves to be recorded. In Ethiopia the situation is somewhat different. Ethiopia had given refuge to the first Muslim refugees fleeing from Meccan persecution in the days of the prophet of Islam. Early Muslim historiography views the Ethiopians with respect because of this initial friendly encounter (which indeed resulted in some religious discussion as well).[6] The contemporary situation, however, is not so peaceful. There is considerable tension between the Christian majority and the Muslim minority. Some groups of Muslims have begun armed action against the government and are seeking secession from Ethiopia. Under the present government, followers of both religions are under considerable pressure and a situation where the history is so promising has in fact become one of gloom.

(b) *Where there is a balance between different religions.* The obvious historic example is the Lebanon. Again, early promise in this context has turned sour. The will and the ability of Christians and Muslims to live together which are mirrored in the Lebanese constitution have been overtaken by events in the Middle East which have shattered Muslim–Christian understanding in the Lebanon. It is important, nevertheless, to remember that not all Christians are party to the conflict and many ecumenical and confessional attempts have been made to foster reconciliation in the nation.

Nigeria, an important province in the Anglican Communion, is another nation where the Christian and Muslim populations are about equal. It seems that Christians in Nigeria, through the 'Islam in Africa' project and by other means, take an intelligent interest in their Muslim fellow citizens and that some form of outreach and ministry to Muslims is still possible. It would be fascinating to see a theology of dialogue emerge from a context such as Nigeria's. How do Nigerians of different faiths coexist together in one nation? How do Muslims live by their Shari'ah without seeking to impose it on others? What freedom of worship and witness does one faith have in areas where the other is predominant? Answers to such questions would provide much food for thought for Christians and Muslims in other situations.

(c) *Where Christians are a minority.* A great deal of very significant inter-faith encounter has taken place in such situations. In India, for example, the incarnational model for such encounter has taken deep root in the Christian tradition, and Christian presence (in the form of Ashrams, for example) in other-faith areas has brought tremendous fruits in terms of increased understanding, mutual stimulus and a common agenda for transformation of society. Many Christians have spent a great part of their lives living in close proximity with (say) Hindus. Often Christians have chosen to live with those of other faiths who are economically depressed or socially oppressed as a sign of solidarity with them and as a way of bringing about meaningful change. They have quite often made a significant impact, and the theology of inter-faith encounter which emerges from such contexts is surely worth a hearing.[7]

As opposed to India, Korea is a country where Christianity has a relatively short history (two hundred years or so at most). Yet it is also undoubtedly a country where the Christian enterprise is flourishing. One of the reasons for this is certainly the fact that during the Japanese occupation Christians steadfastly refused to worship the emperor at Shinto shrines set up by the imperial authorities. Christianity is thus associated in Korea with nationalism, and the affirmation of Christians as to Christian distinctiveness is also seen as an affirmation of Korean-ness.[8] In minority situations the challenge of the Gospel to aspects of other faiths, to syncretism and to debased forms of Christianity is often to the fore and needs to be taken seriously in reflection on inter-faith encounter.

Returning from history to theology, much Anglican thinking on the subject raises certain crucial questions:

(a)   It has to be asked whether our concern for 'inclusiveness', that is to say, a concern for developing a theology which tries to find room for other faiths in the plan of salvation, actually does justice to the distinctiveness of other religions. In other words, non-Christian religions are not simply crypto-Christian religions. They have their own distinct origins, doctrines and rituals which need to be respected and studied for what they are.[9] On the other hand, however, a willingness to enter into dialogue excludes a position which holds to strict autonomy of the different religions to their own histories, faith-systems and ethical emphases.[10] A willingness to enter into dialogue will recognise that religions, although distinct, *are* accountable to each other and are open to scrutiny by all men in terms of values and truths universally recognised as basic to human society. Such a 'mutual reckoning', we have already said, must form a significant part of inter-religious dialogue.[11]

(b)   It is now recognised by a broad spectrum of Christians that Christians and the Church do not have a monopoly over truth and that there is recognition and promotion of truth far beyond the boundaries of the Church. An appeal is sometimes made to the prologue of St John's Gospel (1.4,9) and to Justin Martyr and certain others of the Fathers to show that all men have access to the truth through the *Logos spermatikos* or 'scattered Word' which illuminates human understanding. If by this it is meant that natural man has some knowledge of God and of spiritual matters then this is clearly scriptural teaching (Acts 14.17, Acts 17.22-29, Romans 1–3); but it is equally scriptural teaching that men inevitably corrupt such knowledge of the truth and therefore it cannot save them (Romans 1–3). It needs further to be pointed out that neither in St John nor in the Fathers does the doctrine of the *Logos spermatikos* teach the presence of the Word *in other religions.* In fact Bishop Rudvin has shown that the context in Justin at least is the denial of the truth of other religions, using the Hellenistic philosophers as allies in this area and postulating the work of the *Logos spermatikos* in them as they developed their critique of the religions around them.[12]

(c)   It is held sometimes that various dominical and apostolic encounters with those of other faiths give us 'clues' for inter-religious dialogue. The instances most often quoted are Jesus' encounter with the Syro-Phoenician woman (Mark 7.24-30 and parallels) and with the centurion (Matt. 8.5-13, Luke 7.1-10, John 4.46-53), Peter's encounter with Cornelius (Acts 10–11) and Paul's with the Athenians. As far as the first two examples are concerned, the discipline of redaction criticism compels us to ask the question: why have these incidents been included in the Gospels? The answer that has usually been given to this question is that they were included to point to the approaching universal mission of the Church. In other words, although it is recognised that Jesus' earthly ministry was confined largely to the Jewish nation, already within it, proleptically as it were, there were signs that the preaching of the approaching reign of God would not remain confined to the Jews. Further, they were included to show that the dividing wall of hostility between Jew and non-Jew is broken down in Christ. As the Matthean account of the encounter with the centurion puts it:

> I tell you, many will come from east and west and sit at table with Abraham, Isaac, and Jacob in the kingdom of heaven (Matt. 8.11).

Or as St Paul says:

> For through him we both have access in one Spirit to the Father. So then you are no longer strangers and sojourners, but you are fellow citizens with the saints and members of the household of God (Eph. 2.18-19).

It is somewhat far-fetched to hold that an inter-faith encounter is being portrayed in these incidents. The evangelists' point simply is that response to the Messiah comes from the most unexpected sources, that men and women *despite* their pagan background recognised him. Much is made too of the Cornelius story where a non-Jew is called 'devout' and 'God-fearing'.[13] The whole context of the story, however, shows Cornelius not to have been an adherent of another religion but one of a number of

'God-fearers', i.e. Gentiles who, nevertheless, worshipped the God of Israel, observed the Jewish disciplines of prayer, fasting and almsgiving and only stopped short of circumcision and formal conversion.

Paul's encounter with the Athenians seems to be genuine inter-faith encounter after all, and even Rudvin is forced to acknowledge this.[14] Its significance seems to be that Paul makes a positive evaluation of the 'religiousness' of the Athenians and quotes from what may be regarded as their sacred scriptures, the Poets. On the other hand, his proclamation makes the 'unknown' known, the mystery is made manifest and the *false* aspects of the Athenians' religion (such as idolatry) are condemned.

If this is a model for inter-faith dialogue then unequivocal proclamation must follow positive evaluation even at the risk of jeopardizing the dialogue. Paul is patient in the face of unbelief and even ridicule, he is sympathetic to the spiritual aspirations of his listeners, he is aware of their religious tradition. All these are attitudes in dialogue which deserve commendation. Paul is also clear in his presentation of the apostolic preaching of the death and resurrection of Jesus Christ and this too deserves commendation and imitation.

Interestingly, Jesus' encounter with the Samaritan woman (John 4) and the parable of the Good Samaritan (Luke 10.29-37) are not often mentioned in this context. Yet in the former Jesus is pointing to a knowledge and worship of God which is post-cultic (23,24). Surely this has significance for inter-faith dialogue? Again in the parable of the Good Samaritan the authentically good man is the one furthest removed from orthodox religion. This is obviously significant in the formulation of our views regarding those of other faiths and of no faith.

Elijah's sojourn with the widow of Zarephath (1 Kings 17) and Elisha's healing of Naaman the Syrian (2 Kings 5) are sometimes cited as instances of inter-faith encounter. In Elijah's case it needs to be noted that the whole thrust of his ministry is in his persistent refusal to compromise with Baalism. The Elisha story is more suggestive, for it ends with the prophet giving Naaman permission to continue to participate in the cult of the god Rimmon. Two points have to be made here: first, Naaman asks *pardon* of Yahweh and his prophet for continuing in the worship of Rimmon; secondly, Elisha recognised the social and cultural difficulties facing Naaman and permitted him to be a secret believer. This still occurs, of course, in many cases where those who have come to believe in Christ cannot openly make a declaration because of their social context. The Melchizedek incident (Genesis 14) and the story of Balaam (Numbers 22–24) are certainly a recognition in the Old Testament that God not only speaks to those of other faiths but that *he uses them to speak to us*. This is a somewhat radical but, nevertheless, necessary conclusion from the evidence. It remains true that Israel's openness to the interpretation of authentic religious experience, within it or outside, in categories drawn from other traditions is never allowed to compromise the insistence on divine unity.

(d)   In order to find room for other faiths in the plan and providence of God, attempts have been made to reduce or to do away with the concept of 'Salvation History'. It is felt that Salvation History, by stressing the election of a particular people, 'tribalizes' God and does not permit the emergence of a universalist theology. In Asia it is sometimes said that the other faiths to which Christianity has to relate are 'cosmic' rather than historical and Christianity too must recast its theology in cosmic and a-historical terms. Against this, it has been well said in the Church of England report that the election of the people of God is to be understood as an election for witness and service and leaves no room for pride.[15]

Furthermore, the election is so that the people of God may be 'a light to lighten the Gentiles' (Isa. 42.6, Luke 2.32). Biblical universalism, as it is developed in the prophets and later in the New Testament, is the belief that God's salvation is for all men and that the people of God are agents in conveying this good news to all men. They are not the only agents, of course, for God may work directly in men's hearts and his prevenient grace may cause them to respond to him in repentance and faith. We may agree at once with the Church of England report that God's work is through Christ and that those who respond to it, whether they are conscious of it or not, are responding through Christ and in solidarity with him.[16] In other words, Christ is the locus of the reconciliation; from God to man and from man to God. He is the personification of God's initiative of love and at the same time he is the second Adam who in his radical obedience undoes the effects of the sin of disobedience of the first Adam.

We may go even further than this and say that each group with a language, a culture and a religious tradition has a salvation history. What constitutes such salvation histories can, however, be only determined when there is a normative Salvation History which allows us to determine what is of salvific value in the other traditions. These elements of salvific value may then be regarded as *praeparatio evangelica*. It must, however, be pointed out that it is not necessary for these salvation histories to be entirely congruent with the religious tradition of a people. In fact the salvation history of a people may challenge its religious traditions at important points.

We must reiterate then the 'scandal of particularity' of the Bible but at the same time we must acknowledge God's activity among all peoples and nations, to which the Bible itself bears witness. The particular Salvation History of Israel which is brought to a climax (but not to an end) in the Incarnation, Crucifixion and Resurrection of Our Lord Jesus Christ is a witness to God's desire to restore all men to fellowship with him and allows us to discern where there are signs of response to this divine initiative among other peoples. In the Church, moreover, all men are invited to become part of God's chosen people by baptism into Christ's death and by regeneration into his risen life. Barth makes the important point that election of all others is a participation in Christ's election. All those who open themselves to the work of the Holy Spirit and who accept God's offer of free pardon are elected *in Christ*.[17]

(e)   The rejection of biblical Salvation History as normative for our understanding of the human predicament and the divine initiative is sometimes accompanied by a 'cosmic' or a-historical view of Christ. It is asserted, for example, that the eternal Logos, although supremely manifest in Jesus, is not exhausted by the Jesus of history. He may therefore be revealed in other religious traditions. We have already seen that neither Scripture nor tradition sees the Logos as active in this way. But, further, is it correct to assert, after the Incarnation, activity of the Logos *apart* from the figure of Jesus Christ? We confess after all, the divine-human unity as in the Chalcedonian definition:

> . . . one and the same Christ, Son, Lord, unique; acknowledged in two natures without confusion, without change, without division, without separation — the difference of the natures being by no means taken away because of the union, but rather the distinctive character of each nature being preserved and (each) combining in one Person and hypostasis — not divided or separated into two persons, but one and the same Son and only begotten God, Word, Lord Jesus Christ.

Ignatius had said much the same thing centuries earlier:

> There is one Physician, of flesh and of spirit, originate and unoriginate, God in man, true life in death, Son of Mary and Son of God, first passible and then impassible, Jesus Christ our Lord.[18]

The fact of the matter is that the Word has *become* flesh, not simply manifested itself in flesh. Jesus Christ is the full, definitive and final revelation of God for us. Whatever else may be claimed of God, it is to be judged in the light of this definitive revelation which takes place in the full light of history, though, of course, it points to that which is beyond history. The history of the man Jesus is inescapably, finally and irrevocably tied up with the eternal Word and the one cannot be understood without the other.[19]

(f)   Another curious result of this desire to 'flee' history is to begin to regard God the Holy Spirit as somehow distanced from Sacred History, working as a kind of benign spiritual influence. So the Church of England report can say of the Spirit's work that it is 'unpredictable, culturally and historically indeterminate'.[20] But this is not the Holy Spirit of the Bible, who is associated from the very beginning with the work of Creation, who inspires the prophets, who authenticates the call and ministry of Jesus, who is poured out on the Church, who witnesses to Jesus and who glorifies Jesus. The work of the Spirit in the world seems to be 'prophetic'; so the Spirit convicts this sinful world of its sins, he makes it aware of imminent judgement and also (to those who have ears to hear) of salvation (John 16.7-11). It is the Spirit who convicts a sinner of his sin and makes him alive to God (1 Cor. 2.10f). In this sense an aspect of the work of the Spirit is always ahead of and outside the Church. The Spirit, however, is also continually renewing the Church and equipping it for mission.

So we can say with John Keble:

> It fills the Church of God; it fills
> The sinful world around;
> Only in stubborn hearts and wills
> No place for it is found.

The Spirit is omnipresent because he is God, he is active in the Church and the world, but a reverent study of Scripture and tradition would show that he is not at all unpredictable and indeterminate in his activity. He is faithful, trustworthy and true, he bears definite witness to Jesus Christ the incarnate, crucified and risen Logos, and in all that he does he is faithful to the revelation of the Triune God in Scripture as it has been received, preserved and reflected upon by the community of faith.

(g) The Christian doctrine and practice of the sacraments (particularly the dominical ones of Baptism and Eucharist) raise the question as to how meaningful and profound can be Christian participation in structured inter-faith worship. Baptism is a participation in Christ's death and his resurrection (Col. 2.11-15). This is not participation in some a-historical fertility cult of dying and rising gods. It is participation in a unique event in history, which has supra-historical reverberations, and which is seen as having eternal consequences for the initiate. From the earliest times Christian initiation has been regarded as exclusive in the sense that one could not receive Christian Baptism and also receive initiation in (say) a mystery cult. This still holds true, by and large; one cannot be a Christian and also be a member of another religion (this is not always so of other religions; one can, for example, be Shinto and Buddhist at the same time. The 'jealousy' of the Christian faith is in high profile here). Participation in the Eucharist is also regarded as participation in the once-for-all sacrifice at Calvary which obtains the benefits of Christ's death for us. Again, participation in it precludes participation in the sacrificial rituals of other religions (1 Cor. 10.14-22). In the Muslim context, one is always faced with the pastoral problem of what to say to Christians who want to know whether it is permissible to eat the meat of sacrificial animals at the Muslim feast of 'Id-ul-Adha. The answer that is often given (I believe correctly) is that eating such meat should be avoided, for it is dishonouring to the Eucharist. If we believe that an all-sufficient sacrifice has been offered for us, if we believe that in the Eucharist we are privileged to participate in such a sacrifice, if, moreover, we believe that Scripture and tradition discourage us from participating in the Eucharist as well as in other sacrifices, what choice have we left?

The sacraments then impart a certain exclusive character to Christian commitment since they are regarded as a corporate, mystical participation in events in Sacred History which are regarded as unique. Participation, through the sacraments, in these sacred events has always been regarded as precluding participation in the worship and rituals of other faith-systems.

Just as the sacraments are understood as central to Christian worship, so also is prayer in the name of Jesus and to Jesus (John 16.23-26 is a good example of the former, while Acts 7.59, 1 Cor. 16.22, and Rev. 22.20 are examples of the latter).[21] What can worship mean to a Christian which is not offered in the name of Jesus Christ and to Jesus Christ? The experience of inter-faith worship then, where matters are necessarily reduced to the lowest common denominator, can be a somewhat desolating experience where a person does not encounter the realities of his worship-experience.

The development of a theology of inter-faith dialogue must take into account the varying contexts in which encounter in fact takes place between Christians and those of other faiths; it must take serious account of the distinctive beliefs of other faiths which may, at times, be opposed to cherished Christian beliefs; and it must reflect profoundly on the 'givens' of Scripture and tradition. It is true that authentic contemporary theology can only arise as a result of a creative engagement between the community of faith as it is today and Scripture and tradition. It is also true, however, that the same community of faith accepts certain norms by which its life is ordered and its thought governed. While allowing freedom to theologians to engage with Scripture and tradition on the one hand and with contemporary issues on the other, the community must safeguard the authority of norms on which its existence depends. It is only under such conditions that genuine inter-faith dialogue can take place between Christians and those of other faiths. Such a dialogue would be a source of enrichment for Christians as they expose themselves to other traditions while at the same time it would be an opportunity for humble, loving and serving witness.

FOOTNOTES

[1] S. J. Samartha, *The Hindu Response to the Unbound Christ,* Madras 1974. See also M. M. Thomas, *The Acknowledged Christ of the Indian Renaissance,* London 1969.

[2] V. Samuel and C. Sugden (eds.), *The Gospel among our Hindu Neighbours* (Bangalore 1983), pp. 201ff.

[3] M. Nazir-Ali, *Islam: A Christian Perspective* (Westminster Press 1983), pp. 145ff.

[4] George Bebawi, 'The Future of Christianity in the Middle East', CMS unpublished paper 1985.

[5] The latest example of this, of course, is the report to which this essay is appended.

[6] See further G. Parrinder, *Jesus in the Quran,* London 1965.

[7] In different ways this point is illustrated by Bede Griffiths, *The Marriage of East and West,* London 1982, and V. Samuel and C. Sugden (eds.), op.cit.

[8] D. Kwang-Sun Suh, 'Minjung and Theology in Korea' in *Minjung Theology,* ed. K. Y. Bock (Singapore 1981), pp. 17f.

[9] See for example A. Rudvin, 'The Gospel and Islam: What sort of dialogue is possible?', *Al Mushir,* Autumn 1979 (Rawalpindi), pp. 94ff.

[10] Ninian Smart uses the term 'conceptual fideism' to indicate a position which holds that to understand a faith properly one must belong to it (in J. Hick (ed.), *Truth and Dialogue* (London 1974), pp. 52ff.

[11] K. Cragg, *Muhammad and the Christian: A Question of Response* (New York and London 1984), pp. 12f.

[12] Rudvin, op. cit., pp. 111f.

[13] See pp. 24-26 above.

[14] op.cit., p. 112.

[15] See pp. 16-17 above.

[16] See pp. 25-26 above. Any notion of *earning* salvation, particularly through religious practices, must be carefully excluded. See further C. Sugden, *Christ's Exclusive Claims and Inter-Faith Dialogue* (Nottingham 1985), pp. 13-14 (quoting Sir Norman Anderson).

[17] K. Barth, *Church Dogmatics II, The Doctrine of God 2,* E.T. Edinburgh 1959; cf. Eph. 1.4.

[18] *Epistle to the Ephesians* VII.2.

[19] Rudvin, op.cit., pp. 116f.

[20] See p. 20 above.

[21] O. Cullmann, *Early Christian Worship,* London 1953. See also Cullmann's *Christology of the New Testament* (London 1959), pp. 214f.

AN ANNOTATED BIBLIOGRAPHY

This Bibliography was first published in 1984, for the Church of England.
It has been revised for this edition to mid-1986, adding only publications
from 1984 onwards, and including mainly works published in Britain.
Britain has been a notable source of inter-faith booklets. For books, the
US edition is given where known, but many of the books listed have been
published in the USA and several other countries.

(i)   Booklets to 1984

Guidelines on Dialogue with People of Living Faiths and Ideologies.
WCC, 1979. An outline of the meaning and principles of dialogue, developed over ten years, as a theological basis for thirteen Guidelines
recommended to the churches for study and action.

Kenneth Cracknell, *Why Dialogue?* BCC, 1980.
A first British comment on the WCC *Guidelines,* and commended by the
BCC.

Relations with People of Other Faiths. Guidelines for Dialogue in Britain.
Revised Edition, BCC, 1983.
A sympathetic appreciation of the WCC *Guidelines,* outlining four
principles more directly relevant to Britain. Includes an extremely useful
section on resources for dialogue.

Lesslie Newbigin, *Christian Witness in a Plural Society.* BCC, 1977.
A biblical viewpoint stressing the uniqueness of Christ, and dialogue as
the means of witnessing to Christ.

John V. Taylor, *The Theological Basis of Interfaith Dialogue.* 1977.
Reprinted in Hick and Hebblethwaite (eds.), *Christianity and Other Religions,* see below.
The first Lambeth Interfaith Lecture, setting out some differences and
common ground between the faiths, and pleading for 'patient persis-
tence'.

With People of Other Faiths in Britain. London, United Reformed
Church, 1980.
A Study Handbook for Christians, with local case studies and suggesting
that Christians do not necessarily have all the answers.

Christians and Jews in Britain. London, United Reformed Church, 1983.
A good handbook for understanding issues of Jewish-Christian dialogue,
produced by Christians and Jews working together.

Our Ministry and Other Faiths. A Booklet for Hospital Chaplains.
London, CIO Publishing, 1983.
For hospital chaplains and parish clergy, information about other faiths,
presented for quick reference, with sensitivity.

Can We Pray Together? Guidelines on Worship in a Multi-Faith Society.
BCC, 1983.
Here are many practical suggestions for further action and involvement,
and warnings for the over-enthusiastic.

Kenneth Cracknell (ed.), *Christians and Muslims Talking Together.* BCC,
1984.
This is the distilled wisdom of men and women whose life work has been
to talk with Muslims. A European perspective, translated from the
German.

Christianity and Other Faiths. Exeter, Paternoster Press, 1983.
A short and simple presentation arguing for Christian exclusiveness,
though without arrogance, by a working party for the Evangelical
Alliance chaired by Patrick Sookhdeo.

A Future in Partnership. A Green Paper for discussion published by The
National Society (Church of England) for Promoting Religious Education, 1984.

Schools and Multi-Cultural Education. Church of England Board of
Education, 1984.
A discussion document on an important area.

Christopher Lamb, *Mixed-Faith Marriage: A case for care.* BCC, 1982.
A guide and reference book for those asked to give counsel and advice
about marriages between people who profess different religions.

(ii)   Booklets 1984 onwards

*The Attitude of the Church Towards the Followers of Other Religions.
Reflections and Orientations on Dialogue and Mission.* Secretariat for
Non-Christians, Vatican City, Pentecost 1984.
The Vatican Secretariat, after 20 years experience, offers a document on
Dialogue and Mission, including four different forms of dialogue.

Chris Wright, *Inter Faith Dialogue.* Article in *Anvil,* Vol. 1, No. 3, 1984.
Available as an offprint, with a short reply from Christopher Lamb, from
The Editor, *Anvil,* Trinity College, Bristol, BS9 1JW, England. The first
and most detailed analysis of *Towards a Theology for Inter-Faith
Dialogue,* from a Conservative Evangelical standpoint.

Christopher Sugden, *Christ's Exclusive Claims and Inter-Faith Dialogue,*
Grove Pastoral Series No. 22. Grove Books, Bramcote, Notts. 1985.
Another detailed analysis, written at the request of the Church of
England Evangelical Council, with a Bibliography.

Journey of Discovery. An approach to the World Faiths. London, United
Reformed Church, 1985.
To help people of local churches meet people of other faiths.

Kenneth Leech (ed.), *Theology & Racism - 1. The Bible, Racism and Anti-Semitism*. London, Church of England Board for Social Responsibility, 1985.
Four writers on anti-Semitism in Christian theology.

Theology & Racism - 2. Inheritors Together, Black people in the Church of England. London, Church of England Board for Social Responsibility, 1985. Four more writers in this new series.

Inter-Faith Dialogue in the Diocese of London. 1986. Available from London Diocesan House, 30 Causton Street, London SW1P 4AU.
The Report of a working party chaired by Richard Harries. One diocese considering positively *Towards a Theology for Inter-Faith Dialogue*.

Kenneth Cracknell and Christopher Lamb, *Theology on Full Alert*. Revised and Enlarged Edition, BCC, 1986.
Stories, resources, and discussion of issues for everyone in theological education in a religiously plural world.

(iii)   Books to 1984

Gerald H. Anderson and Thomas F. Stransky (eds.), *Christ's Lordship and Religious Pluralism*. Maryknoll, NY, Orbis Books, 1981. London, SPCK, 1983.
An interesting account of different Christian viewpoints arguing with one another.

John Bowker, *Worlds of Faith*. London, British Broadcasting Corporation, 1983.
Religious belief and practice in Britain today, based on over a hundred interviews with members of six faiths for a BBC Radio series.

Arnulf Camps, *Partners in Dialogue: Christianity and Other World Religions*. Maryknoll, NY, Orbis Books, 1983.
Excellent survey of the whole area by a leading Dutch Roman Catholic missionary thinker. Three books translated from the Dutch into one volume.

Bede Griffiths, *The Marriage of East and West*. London, Collins, 1982.
The fruit of many years living in Indian culture; a Benedictine monk outlines how the truths of Christianity and Hinduism can be seen as complementary while retaining the uniqueness of Christ.

John Hick, *God Has Many Names*. London, Macmillan, 1980. Philadelphia, Westminster Press, 1982.
A collection of essays giving ready access to a Pluralist theory in the relations between the faiths. An Appendix by Kenneth Cracknell on the growth of inter-faith work in Britain up to 1980.

John Hick and Brian Hebblethwaite (eds.), *Christianity and Other Religions. Selected Readings.* London, Collins, Fount Paperbacks, 1980.
A collection of essays from major theologians since 1923, offering a variety of solutions to the problems of inter-faith meeting.

Lesslie Newbigin, *The Open Secret. Sketches for a Missionary Theology.* London, SPCK, 1978. Grand Rapids, Michigan, Eerdmans, 1978.
A statement from a well-known British writer in defence of the uniqueness of Christ while being sympathetic to the other faiths.

Raimundo Panikkar, *The Unknown Christ of Hinduism.* Revised and Enlarged Edition, London, Darton, Longman & Todd, 1981; Maryknoll, NY, Orbis Books, 1981.
A scholarly appreciation by a Catholic writer who views the spirit of Christ at work but hidden in other faiths. Modified since the first edition.

Alan Race, *Christians and Religious Pluralism. Patterns in the Christian Theology of Religions.* London, SCM Press, 1983.
An analysis of the range of Christian theories now operating in response to the awareness of many faiths and an attempt to classify them.

John A. T. Robinson, *Truth is Two-Eyed.* London, SCM Press, 1979.
An argument for the complementarity between the prophetic and mystical religious traditions whilst retaining the superiority of Christ.

Wilfred Cantwell Smith, *Towards a World Theology.* London, Macmillan, 1981.
A technical essay arguing that all faiths reflect the operation of the spirit of God in different cultural forms, and pleading for the end of isolation in theological work.

(iv)   Books 1984 onwards

Norman Anderson, *Christianity and World Religions. The Challenge of Pluralism.* London, Inter-Varsity Press, 1984.
A defence of the uniqueness of Christianity from the standpoint of the Incarnation. Completely revised edition of *Christianity and Comparative Religion,* 1971.

Wesley Ariarajah, *The Bible and People of Other Faiths.* WCC Risk Book Series, 1985. Co-published with the WSCF Asia/Pacific Region, Hong Kong.
The Director of the Dialogue Sub-unit of the World Council of Churches, explaining the biblical issues.

Kenneth Cracknell, *Towards a New Relationship. Christians and People of Other Faith.* London, Epworth Press, 1986.
Personal, biblical and theological reflections from the author's experience, since 1978, as the Executive Secretary of the Committee for Relations

with People of Other Faiths, of the British Council of Churches. Bibliographical notes.

Kenneth Cragg, *The Call of the Minaret*. 2nd Edition Revised and Enlarged. London, Collins, 1986.
The classic work of the great English student of Islam, first published in 1956.

Gavin D'Costa, *Theology and Religious Pluralism*. Oxford, Blackwell, 1986.
An Indian Roman Catholic, born in East Africa, teaching in London, presents John Hick, Hendrik Kraemer and Karl Rahner as representatives of the Pluralist, Exclusivist and Inclusivist paradigms for a theology of religions.

Roger Hooker and Christopher Lamb, *Love the Stranger. Ministry in Multi-Faith Areas*. London, SPCK, 1986.
To be published in October 1986. The fruits of a combination of scholarship and ministry in and around Birmingham.

Edward J. Hughes, *Wilfred Cantwell Smith. A Theology for the World*. London, SCM Press, 1986.
Introducing the Canadian scholar's work to a wider public, from his classic *The Meaning and End of Religion* to the possibilities for a world theology.

Paul F. Knitter, *No Other Name? A Critical Survey of Christian Attitudes Toward the World Religions*. London, SCM Press, 1985.
The broadest survey yet of the different attitudes, more detailed and nuanced than either Race or D'Costa, by an American Roman Catholic Professor of Theology.

Christopher Lamb, *Belief in a Mixed Society*. Lion Publishing, 1985.
How can Christians live with other faiths in Britain? Specific issues in everyday life: education, food, marriage and family, and many others.

Stephen Neill, *Crises of Belief. The Christian Dialogue with Faith and No Faith*. London, Hodder & Stoughton, 1984.
An analysis of the great world faiths, raising questions from a Christian perspective to each faith in turn. Replaces his *Christian Faith and Other Faiths,* 1970.